MONKEY JOY

RETURN TO YOUR PRIMAL JOY

JEN WARD

🐢 Created with Vellum

CONTENTS

1. Joy   1
2. Resonating With Love   12
3. Expansion Of Heaven   28
4. Freedom   33
5. Healing   47
6. Spiritual Transformation   65
7. Beyond All Illusion   84
8. Companionship   108
9. Creativity   125
10. Changing The Algorithms Of Life   135
11. Manifesting Peace   157
12. Assisting Mass Awakening   168
13. The Energetic Cleanse   188

Glossary of Terms   191
About the Author   195
Also By Jen Ward   197

JOY

⮾

Awakened People
Awakened people are like Stars in the Sky. They are not meant to cluster in a group. In doing so, they may bicker about the coordinates that sustain them, and which one is brightest. The awakened are meant to spread themselves across the galaxy and each be a beacon for others in the darkness.

Please Adam, Eat That Apple

The visions of the future of the world going down in destruction are obsolete. Visionaries could only see a slanted vision from a male point of view. This means the best of them that you have built your spiritual disciplines around.

They were unable to see the shifts in the reality itself, caused by the empowerment of female energy. This showed in their negative view of women leaders. What we are experiencing now is a whole shift of vantage point and empowerment that visionaries of the past couldn't fathom.

The truth is: The shift in consciousness caused by female empowerment is what saves the planet. Things are shifting so quickly. We are all getting a tutorial in how idiotic and corrupt governing parties are that are devoid of female energy. This includes compassion, kindness and expansive inclusiveness.

It is no accident that I do such dynamic energy work and share such wise insights while in a female body. It is no accident that so many wise and empowered people are incarnating in female bodies. The world is desperate for what others and I offer.

What you are seeing now is consciousness outgrowing the primal conditioning that women are evil. I never understood why Eve was the bad guy for bringing Adam self-awareness. The Garden of Eden represents the apathy and ignorance that we have tolerated. The snake represents our kundalini energy or tapping into our Higher Truth.

Right now, Adam is being urged to eat the apple. Of course we are naked when we have little understanding of ourselves as energy beings. Our subtle senses need to be reengaged so that we can expand our consciousness. This is where we are at. This is what conventional religion created by male dominance has been trying to prevent. But it is inevitable.

Go back to all that we have been conditioned to believe. Reassess all the demonizing of women that is threaded through our history. See that the corruption that is coming to the head was always working to thwart our expansion into female empowerment.

In all you do, think, intend and believe, coax Adam to eat that apple. Please Adam, for humanity's sake, please eat that apple. I have a lot to offer humanity. So do you. We do it in sisterhood, by sharing everything we are and know as intended for a favorite sister. The days of besting and subjugating our brother is over. This message is the key to awakening for all of humanity.

Why Are You Here?

So many people are just watching the news and lamenting what a shitty place this world is. They use what little energy they have left to piss and moan about the state of affairs. Yet when anyone comes along who really has the intention of helping the uplifting of humanity, they get mercilessly attacked. Why?

People are terrified of fulfilling their soul contract. They are afraid to even fathom who they are beyond the illusion of this time and space. Do we really believe we just came here to lament over wanting more love and money most of our days? Then when all hope of fulfilling our dreams of more love and money evaporate, we turn our energy to the fear of death?

Are we still really so manipulated? Can't we see breaks in the tapestry of illusion? If God is love, why are we so trained to hate? Why do our particular beliefs forbid us from questioning? If the factions of truth are in charge, why is there so much suffering in the world? Why do the people who come here to help uplift humanity, like myself, meet so much derision?

Who are you as a spiritual being? I get attacked so many times by people who are on a supposed spiritual path and are so interested in what I share. When I say attacked, I am not talking about snide comments. I am talking about literal energetic attacks beyond this world of illusion. They want me gone. They demonize my message so that others avoid truth.

They like what I say for a while and if I say one thing that doesn't fit with their understanding, they resent me and end up attacking or avoiding me like the plague. They end up aligning with a more comfortable path where one will instill dominance and tell them what to do, all the while making them believe that they are empowering them.

They keep them trapped in a mental holding cell and removed from their purpose. They are part of the spiritual elite that believe they know what is best for everyone but want to keep the masses ignorant of truth so they can be superior.

What I do here is share truth beyond the veil of illusion. I take very complicated concepts for those entrenched in illusion and allow truth to filter back into their very conditioned physical brain. In energy, some are cowering and shackled. But the truth I share literally sets them free. I give them taps to help them find love and attract money, but I am doing more. Love and money are the dangling carrots. They will be more free to receive them. But I am using their human desire for love and money to show them how to empower themselves once again.

It has been a long time, in a reality very far away, that most of you have really felt empowered. This desire plays out in your preferences for war games and movies. It also plays out in a desire to know your purpose. At the core, you know this world is not fulfilling. The illusion provided has run its course. At one time you thought it was only you who was feeling this way. Now you are starting to understand through social media that there is a universal desperation to be empowered.

Because there are still so few of us living our soul contract, we get attacked for trying to break the programming and conditioning that occurs. You have even experienced such shifts in the algorithms of social media. The more that we share positive beneficial posts to support each other, the less our posts are shared. That is not an accident. That is by design by factions that wish to use social media to keep us divided rather than allow us to realize our empowerment.

If any of this resonates, please do the exercise of taps below. If you have been wondering what your life purpose is, please do these taps. If you worry about the suffering of others and are tired of feeling helpless, please do these taps. If you have outgrown the belief systems of group factions that seem to teach hate instead of love, please do these taps. If you have benefited from anything I have posted and it has stirred something within you about your own empowerment, please do these taps.

As more of you awaken and step up to your responsibilities as an empowered being, the easier it will get for all to be empowered. The fear will dry up and also more of the illusion. There will be more of a place for truth, love, kindness and creativity in the world as universal practices, and not just to line the pockets of the entitled.

(Say each statement three times while tapping on your head and say a fourth time while tapping on your chest.)

"I do these taps for myself and as a surrogate for all souls; in all moments."

"I make space in all worlds to activate the fulfillment of my soul's contract; in all moments."

"I remove all blockages in all worlds to the activation of the fulfillment of my soul's contract; in all moments."

"I open all portals in all worlds to the activation of the fulfillment of my soul's contract; in all moments."

"I eliminate the first cause in the deactivation of the fulfillment of my soul's contract; in all moments."

"I stretch my capacity to activate and follow through with the fulfillment of my soul's contract; in all moments."

"I am centered and empowered in the activation and fulfillment of my soul's contract; in all moments."

"I resonate, emanate and am interconnected with all life in the activation of my soul's contract; in all moments."

After you have done these taps, please leave a message that you have done them so others may gain the incentive to do them as well. So many people are looking on, yet hesitant to do the actual tapping. The tapping is a method to assist the individuals in getting past their resistance to truth. Not wanting to actually do the taps is the conditioning that needs to be penetrated. The tapping does this.

ACTIVATE *Your Soul Contract*

So many people are unhappy and feel unfulfilled because they have in some way deactivated their soul contract. The soul contract is your true purpose as an energetic being. All your strengths and abilities are utilized to direct as many souls back to Source as possible. Wishing to fulfill your soul contract is reflected in people's desire to know their life's purpose and why they are truly here.

(Say each statement three times while tapping on your head and say a fourth time while tapping on your chest.)

"I make space in all worlds to fulfill my soul contract; in all moments."

"I release all hesitancy in fulfilling my soul contract; in all moments."

"I eliminate the first cause in deactivating my soul contract; in all moments."

"I remove all blockages to fulfilling my soul contract; in all moments."

"I stretch my capacity to fulfill my soul contract; in all moments."

"I activate my soul contract; in all moments."

"I am centered and empowered in fulfilling my soul contract; in all moments."

"I resonate, emanate and am interconnected with all life in the fulfillment of my soul contract; in all moments."

"I am centered and empowered in fulfilling my soul contract; in all moments."

"I resonate, emanate and am interconnected with all life in the fulfillment of my soul contract; in all moments."

ENERGY, *Chakras and God*

Energy spirals. Its flow is not as linear as conceptualized. Maybe when you visualize it coming into the body just through the top of the head and going right down, you are doing yourself a disservice. Maybe you are thwarting the natural flow of energy in some way.

Chakras are not linear. They do not just have an opening at the top where they accept energy in. They accept energy in from all directions. Think of a disco ball. But instead of just throwing out rays of light, it accepts energy from all directions.

The way to more accurately visualize the chakras is like a wand on a cotton candy machine that collects all the sugar fluff that collects around the edge of the barrel. Except that the wand works in a multidimensional sort of way instead of a flat plane surface. The chakras are reaching out and collecting energy in all directions. It is a very active process.

The way you enter and leave the body is through a spiral. That is why when you are lying down to sleep, all the images come from the day, and then more abstract images. The energy of you is spiraling out of the body in a gentle way. The same is true when you are waking up and it takes you a few tries to wake up. The energy of you is spiraling in.

When you wake up really quickly, you are being slammed into the body and it can lead to a headache or grouchiness when awakening. Imagine a big jet airplane slamming into a wall. That is what you are doing when you wake up too quickly. When you think you are awake, lie there for a while and literally collect yourself. Since the astral plane is so close to the physical plane, it may seem like you are back in the body but may be hovering.

When you visualize energy coming into you, see it like sideways rain flooding into you from every direction. See the chakras as active receiving systems with intelligence and purpose rather than stationary globes. They attract energy into the body within a certain range of vibration which is depicted by the color of energy collected.

The colors of the chakras are not just a color-coding system. It is the actual color vibration of the energy that you are collecting and drawing in. The color of your vegetables depicts what vibration of energy they are collecting. So, if you know that you are weak in one particular chakra, take in the energy the body is lacking through that weak chakra by eating vegetables of that color or even wearing clothes of that color as well.

God is energy. Understanding energy helps in understanding God. God is not in a way station out in the sky somewhere. God is meeting us every day in every way and in every form. Every single person, place or thing is God meeting us in different ways to teach us how dynamic we really are. If you don't like what life is showing you, change your agreement with the people and situations around you.

The more that you treat God as an abstract concept to send your energy to and to receive it at its will, the more room to fail in being empowered there is. The more that you have an interactive relation-ship with God and see every living being as a reflection of God and an ambassador of God's love, the more you can hone your understanding of God, the more opportunities to partake of God's love.

God is bombarding you with experiences, lessons, private time, one-on-one learning and a constant barrage of love. Simply to empower you. Everyone receives the lessons they need to realize themselves as dynamic and empowered. Receiving a goody bag of materialism is such a low bar of receiving. Look at the actions of the filthy rich. They will have to live with the despicable consequences of their spiritual lessons for lifetimes to come.

We who serve, we who love all, we who are empathic to the plights of others, we who use our gifts to uplift others in some way are inter-acting with God every day. The more your thoughts, deeds and purpose take in the lessons and use them to create a greater outflow of energy to assist others, then the more you are embracing your true nature as an atom of God.

When you are no longer passive in your concept of God, but active, you have gained much insight into your true nature.

An Aversion to Awakening

Someone was having a strong reaction to doing the Spiritual Freedom Taps (SFT) taps that were freeing her. She started feeling like she was vomiting tar-like energy (she was) and it caused a negative emotional and physical reaction in her. This is basically why I wrote them.

That is actually an exciting thing. It is releasing the trauma of life-times of slavery and misery. There are a lot of psychic energies that are trying one last stand to keep people enslaved. They are making people feel crazy as they start to awaken. These energies have no power of themselves anymore. The only 'in' they have is to convince you that you are overwhelmed by the process of awakening or that you are somehow going crazy, or that doing the taps is bad. It is an old shtick.

The discomfort of awakening may be there because the forces that have held each human in limited positions have been working on the individual psyche to turn on itself. It is the same way that unworthi-ness is programmed into us, but even worse. We believe we are crazy or that something bad is going to happen if we break from the human conditioning and rise to the level of our possible empowerment.

The best way to deal with the freak-out that happens as you start to awaken is to take a non-reactive stance. Stop identifying with the feelings and the subtle energies that are working to create a more empowering equilibrium. Watch as the negative engrams are pulled from you. Don't identify with them as they go. Just let them be peeled away.

Become the observer of the process, like watching clouds go by. Realize that this is not only happening to you, but others are dealing with the same experience as well. You are not alone in your feelings of isolation and overwhelming self-reflection. They are universal. You are tapped into the collective more than ever

Also, understand that whatever you are experiencing, I and perhaps others have already experienced it as well. It is a formula experience to awakening. Awakening is inevitable since we didn't come into existence merely to move around a broom and scrounge for money and love.

I can assist you inwardly. It is something that others have reported that I have done. I may not be conscious of the details. There are so many of you now awakening. But I can perceive in energy and can assist beyond the limitations of the limited body. More and more I am getting comfortable mentioning this because more people tell me that I have assisted them.

I tried to figure out the process with a linear understanding. What I come up with is the love. Love comes to you and assists, and if your mind needs it to take a personal form to have it feel personal, then it will. Whatever form it takes, in purity it is love and not something or someone to be worshiped.

It is part of the human conditioning to want to give your power away. So, the very last trick that the limited psyche has to keep you limited is to have you glom on to whatever symbol your mind uses to represent expansive Divine Love. It is the last-ditch effort to try and keep you entrenched to a limited state of consciousness.

That is why it is silly to fight over who is God. God is Love. Love will take any form that you need it to take, to comfort you in your personal realm. Love can come in any form. You are loved. You are worthy and you are outgrowing all programming that tells you that you are not.

MONKEY JOY

A client came to me disturbed by threats from her ex-husband's family. It was causing a great reaction in her. They had threatened to take her home from her. Immediately my inner vision opened up to a scenario in a past life where she was a Hun. Her group had conquered a village and she was in the midst of them. She was the one who was threatening their well-being. The mere 'memory' of her as the aggressor switched her out of victim mode so she was receptive for what came next.

In that time, they surrounded her and wore her down until one of them was able to pierce him (she was male) with a penetrating spear to the spine. I felt the blow.

"Do you feel that pain on the right side of your lower spine?" I asked. She did. That was where a debilitating blow had landed in her body in that past life. It was what we were releasing, I felt the move through her hip area and an agility return that was missing. She confirmed that although she was very agile, her lower lumbar was always locked. She was amazed. She felt the shift.

The energy continued to move down into her tailbone. I felt her have a tail. Another scene opened up. She was in a jungle in a monkey body, and those from the village from the past image were there as well, including her ex in-laws in the present life. They were a different tribe of monkeys.

In that scenario, she had lost her monkey family and was taken in by a male in the group. She wasn't totally accepted and existed on the fringe of their group. It was a lonely and isolating existence that ended in tragedy. Before encountering this group of monkeys, she was very happy. She exuded a joy of trusting exuberance. In her session, it was time for her to return to that state. She was ready to recapture her monkey joy.

In the session, we did a bunch of energy work where we balanced the transactions between her and the group. It is like energetically balancing the karmic books so that all debts are considered paid back on both sides. There is no need to continue rehashing old debts that play out as petty issues. (It is interesting to watch how the sessions play out in the client's life afterwards.)

We returned the woman to her monkey joy with the added bonus of all the insights she had learned since that naive state. It is a wonderful experience to return to joy after forgetting what it feels like to be imbued in it. It is my hope to assist as many as I can to return to their monkey joy!

RESONATING WITH LOVE

he Cleansing Process
    You see all these spiritual diagrams of light coming into the top of the head. It is not so linear. Light, love and awareness don't bottleneck at the top of the head. That may be one collection center, but so is every cell at all different vibrations. The body is bombarded in light from all directions. It is in a perpetual wash cycle of cleansing and rejuvenation.

    Thinking of light only coming into the body from the top of the head is a means of rejecting one's own rejuvenation. Feel yourself immersed in the cleansing cycle of perpetual love through light and celestial music. Stop limiting what you will accept.

ALL HEARTS LEAD *to Love*

How do you measure your spiritual advancement without understanding that you are an eternal being that has lived many lives and has experienced many different realities? It would be like judging a road trip by what transpired in just one town. Or gauging your success by one small chapter of your life.

    The people who are more open, compassionate and aware are the ones who accept themselves as an eternal being. They understand that those who look like failures under society's scrutiny could be resting from an experience that doesn't touch these realms. Perhaps the underachiever has just fought a heroic battle in their past life and existing here under any conditions is all that they can handle.

Who are we to judge? Unless we view life from an unfiltered awareness beyond a physical belief system, we cannot begin to fathom. Perhaps the most adamant atheist merely resents giving their lifeblood lifetime after lifetime for a petty assessment of God. This is what the thousand years of crusades were about: forcing others to believe as the ruling faction, or to die in battle for what is most sacred to them.

We see these squabbles play out day in and day out in politics and social affairs. It is those of us who have suffered enough who are able to allow those past traumas to bleed through to this present life. We are the ones that refuse to inflict what we have endured onto others.

Those of us who have remembered such things must come to our heart of understanding and stop being squelched of our expansiveness by an outmoded ideology. We have all lived many lives. We must start to listen to our own inner promptings when it comes to compassion, kindness and caring. We must stop echoing the trauma and mistakes of past eras.

It is only in expanding the consciousness of our own understanding can we expand the consciousness of humanity as a whole. We are the saviors of tomorrow. We are the saviors of today. To deny this in ourselves is to deny it to all. That is how important we are. We all are. All hearts lead to Love.

Who, What, and Where Is Love?

Love speaks through the quietude of the moment. It is the very pulse of the heartbeat of Life. Love is the buzzing you hear in your ear that reminds you that there are realms of existence beyond the veil of the illusion of this life.

Love is the wave of gratitude that overcomes you when there is the deep sense of resolve in your day that life is manageable; when your loved ones are safe and fed and you are deemed a proficient provider of their calm.

Love is the magnetic pull between two hearts that are compelled to press together in an attempt to merge as one. It is the mingling of two energies with no deference to boundaries or defenses. It is building a life around this vortex of attraction and extending an arm of it out through the adding of children, fur babies or foliage.

Love is the ability to care for any child of life as if it too had passed through your body and suckled at your breast. It is to defend the innocent as an abstract as well as in each new tender face, limb or experience.

Love is to feel, through your own body sensors, the pain of any stranger who happens along on your path of life. Love is to cry the tears of a stranger you will never meet as you lie in your own bed and deem them your own. Love is to feel the plight of others and to lighten their load by purging out the grief that they, in the moment, do not have the luxury to expel.

Love is the call in the dark that speaks truth to any question that you ask it. It is the wisdom that lies just beyond the clouds of illusion and beckons you to forgo the judgment and the reactionary affront and to listen to the heartbeat of humanity as it rests in all individuals who accompany you in the experience of existing.

Love is seeing God in the eyes of each being and paying homage to Its essence through your acts of kindness. It is creating an altar out of each moment and using each utterance of communication with others as a prayer that simply says, "Thy will be done."

To treat Earth as if it were heaven because it is, and to realize that heaven is not a place but a state of consciousness that you are the caretaker of through your humble service to others. Knowing that humility is not a state of unworthiness or depravity but a bold adventurous state that you are an open gateway for all others to see such exuberance in themselves.

Love is seeing your own embodiment not as a dead vessel but a mini world where you yourself are the God Awareness. Seeing each cell as an eager little foot soldier anxious to please, and to remember to say thank you for all that it does to maintain the sovereignty of you.

Love is to forgo calling your heart 'broken' for merely a petty emotion or calling your whole self 'fat' or other unworthy statements. To realize that anything your body experiences is to serve the whole and not to cause you displeasure. Love is to know that when your body cries out in pain, it is desperate for a validation that the surface mind has refused to give.

Love is dipping into the depth of yourself, like dipping into a reflecting pond and experiencing the ecosystem that is cunningly concealed from the glass-like surface of the outer facade. It is recognizing that the life within is a reflection of the world without, and to appreciate one is symbiotic to appreciating the other.

Love is to know that a great way to heal the world is to heal the misgivings within the self, and vice versa. The more we expand our compassion for life, the more we expand the boundaries of self. We no longer think of ourselves as a finite container with walls of skin but as an emanation of light and a frequency of sound woven into the illusion of form.

We are a galaxy and an orchestra, a secret and a storm. We are the Source of Light and a mere ember always extending our wick to light into blaze all others so they can see themselves with such gusto. We are the Infinite playing the game of illusion, pretending to be insignificant so we can realize the depth of ourselves while immersed in the quagmire of illusion, pain and desire.

Love is the process of being inundated with such illusion of need and shredding the paper facade to realize the incredible empowerment that is our true state. Love is to see, feel and believe ourselves to be the embodiment of love and to extend it out to all others through our kindness and benevolence to all those trapped in the illusion of this world.

Love is the noun that regenerates itself through being a verb. Regenerates all life through its appreciation of it and acceptance of the perfectly imperfect. Love is the beginning meeting its fate through a perpetual state of expansion and acceptance. Realizing that the concept of a fate or an ending other than perpetual growth is merely another turn in the spiral in the expansion of understanding the self as more love.

When all this is realized, all illusion of ego and false self will fall away, and all experiences will merely be Love meeting itself in every situation. As the eyes and all other perceptions become consumed with their true nature, the dross will dissipate, and the perceptions of the small self will be aligned with the awareness of God's Love, and all individuals will realize that they themselves are breathing, living embodiments of Love.

TAPPING *into Your God Self*

The concept of God has to be Universally upgraded from being a man in the clouds. This deference to a lofty old white man is reflected in our outmoded governing body of bloated, entitled, old white men.

How about thinking of God as the intangible part of yourself that you are only limited in knowing because of the limitations of your physical apparatus. God is the invisible aspect of yourself that knows all, sees all and experiences all.

Some people who call themselves empaths, or are tapping into profound truths and have incredible compassion, are blurring the lines between their physical self and their own omniscience as a spiritual being. They get a sense of their own God-Self calling to them beyond the veil of the physical realm.

Accepting yourself as a living, breathing aspect of God affords one great peripheral benefits. If you know yourself to be an expression of God, then it just makes sense that everyone else is an expression of God as well.

Instead of needing to flock to a building to kneel at the altar of God, you can know that you meet God a million times a day. You are in sacred communion every time you assist another being and make their sense of self feel more fulfilled. At first, it is done in grand gestures to stroke one's own ego. But when you get to the point where you are consumed with loving God through empowering God in all forms, then you most likely will have a sense of your own empowerment.

The oxymoron in this understanding is that those who deem themselves the most devout are the ones who damage the God qualities in others the most. Besting others is a demonstrative act of the physicality of self, but not necessary from the God side. Also, judgment and adherence to religious mandates crush the spirit in others. Many of the most sacred texts have been edited throughout the years by entitled men.

They support and perpetuate an understanding of God that was forged in fear during the Dark Ages. These are the mandates that actually prevent people from knowing their God-Self. It is an embedded threat in any religion or spiritual group that prevents them from overstepping their boundaries by questioning the mandates laid out.

How long are humans going to keep falling for it? If the tenets of their faith of choice were so empowering, then we would see love, kindness and truth everywhere. There would be less of a drive to be better than others. What is the difference if the God in them or the God in you is empowered? God is God and we are all God Stuff, so assisting others is a form of worship.

That is why it feels so good to help others. Helping others is us brushing up against our greatness. Besting others outside of friendly competition is going in the opposite direction. Needing to be the best is feeding the ego. The true self is the aspect of you that has been trampled on all sides yet is still compelled to love.

RECONNECTING the Circuit

Two weeks back my friend was devastated. The tree that she had struck up a friendship with had been cut down. To her and me, it is so silly that people think of trees as lifeless objects. They are the most giving, nurturing beings on the planet. They are the closet example that we have of sacred selflessness on the planet. They are abused, neglected, desecrated and destroyed at every turn and yet they continue to give effortlessly and completely of themselves.

This tree would comfort her as she walked her dogs and reached out to her with its wisdom. The tree knew of her work with me in creating a higher vibration on the planet and her help in publishing the book *Wisdom of the Trees* that I wrote. They know of the work we do in helping others understand that trees are not inanimate objects. Trees appreciate being appreciated.

My friend Therese would tell me things that seemed very truthful and profound. This tree had taken her under its wings and was assisting her in understanding greater truths. It was amazing to see Therese open up to great wisdom. It was like she had a mother figure in her life again. It is my intention for everyone to have an incredible understanding for life and the feeling of being loved and valuable. Apparently, it is the tree's intention as well.

When Therese picked me up at my house, she was very sad. She couldn't hide it. She tried to. She knows how deeply I feel things and she was trying to prevent me from feeling her pain. Because she realizes with me, that feeling the pain of someone else is the gateway for me to feel the pain of all the suffering of the world at once. It is excruciating.

That is why, when I assist anyone, I ask them not to give me details. I don't want to feel their emotional pain because then I will inadvertently be tapped into all the pain and suffering in the world all at once and it is too much. It is too much for the human psyche to handle. That is why anyone who works at the level of healing that I work at has to remain detached and removed. It is not because I don't care; it is because I care too much.

She and I were very sad about the tree. The neighbors decided to cut down this very beautiful healthy Sycamore tree that was a focal point in the neighborhood. It was a selfish and myopic decision to cut down the tree that I don't think individuals should be allowed to make. Trees that contribute so much to our environment and sanity should be given citizenship. People shouldn't be allowed to randomly cut them down.

Therese and her husband took turns trying to talk the neighbors out of cutting down the tree. They had no good reason. But they were adamant that the tree had to go. To Therese and me, the cutting down of the tree felt like a personal assault on her. She has witnessed the psychic assaults that I have endured for my work to bring more truth to the world.

It has been a shocking education for her to see what someone who comes here to truly serve endures. The cutting down of the tree that had come to nurture and comfort her seemed personal on some subtle level as well. It was not an accident that I had been compelled to spend time with her that day. Even though I was reeling from the repercussions of dissipating psychic forces, I was drawn to help her.

As we were driving around, a means to make this situation right came to me (probably from the tree). I know how trees communicate through their rooting system. Trees don't die just because their trunk is cut down. Their whole rooting system is still intact, so they are still alive. Therese's majestic friend was not dead. It was just limited for now.

We got the idea to go to the nearest nursery and buy a Sycamore tree to plant on Therese's property just about four feet from the tree that was cut down. I was instructed that the younger tree would be planted over the rooting system of the old tree and the old tree could mingle its consciousness with the new tree. It would then still have the wonderful vantage point that it had enjoyed in the neighborhood.

Therese and I just so happened to be driving by a nursery that had been very helpful the year before when purchasing our potted Gaia tree for the Winter Solstice. They just so happened to have Sycamore trees. It felt that there was a particular tree that was speaking to us to take on this new adventure. At first, the trees saleswoman showed us were either too expensive or too young.

As Therese was looking through the younger trees, the saleswoman seemed to be called back to a mid-range priced tree. It was about ten feet tall. It was the one. The bark seemed like it had similar markings to the one cut down. We could feel the love and approval.

The nursery could deliver it and plant it that Wednesday. The morning of the planting, I was compelled to be present as they planted the new tree. As I let my dogs run in Therese's back yard, I got a calming sense of peace and reverence from the trees out back. Trees are the most incredible healers. They literally keep humans sane by extracting the stagnant energy they collect and replacing it with a clarity and peace. The trees at Therese's house were grateful for my understanding of them. They were about to give me even greater truth about themselves.

I know how all trees communicate through their rooting system. It is similar to how humans connect through social media. The reason why trees are so present with me is because I am present with them. If someone isn't present with a tree, the tree will be despondent to them. The same way a teenager on a video game will seem inanimate. That is how trees show up for someone who doesn't value them. The tree's awareness is in the ground with the other trees unless we make an attempt to engage them.

The trees wanted to show me even greater truth. They told me to go into the front yard where the new tree was being planted. There were amazing huge Sycamores in the other yards of the neighbors. The tree that was cut down was one in a circuit of trees that connect to each other. With the one tree cut down, there was a disconnect in the lines of communications between the trees.

They showed me the analogy of how when one light blows out on an old set of Christmas lights, the whole string of lights goes out. They said it was similar to the trees' communication line. The ignorant people who cut down the healthy majestic tree not only killed a sentient being, they also interfered in a whole circuit of communicating trees in the community. When we planted the new tree, the trees showed me how it reconnected their communication. It was like the trees were each other's support system.

It made perfect sense to me because I have seen trees that were not around other trees and they do seem taxed in a way. The Sycamores in this neighborhood were gushing with vitality. And when the new tree was planted, they all reconnected in a special way. They wanted me to have that understanding for helping them. They even explained to me that different types of trees speak slightly different languages than the others. Sycamore trees speak more fluently to other Sycamore trees.

As soon as the tree was planted, the love was flowing. As soon as Therese picked out the tree from the nursery, the whole experience changed from devastation to empowerment. The energy of Therese's tree friend is still with her and it is expounded by the addition of the new tree and her willingness to care so deeply for the tree folk.

If anyone is feeling lonely or depressed, it is because they are not spending time with their tree family. Once someone experiences the love and wisdom of the trees, it will be impossible to imagine life without it.

Stop Cursing Humanity

The vibrations of the world are changing. People are becoming more open-minded and open-hearted through osmosis. It is important to recognize your own growth of awareness so as not to curse others as hopeless. If you have changed at all, allow that same courtesy to others.

Thinking that those who are close-minded are beyond reaching, is a curse on them. It's a plague on awakening. The more we all hold space for others to surprise us in their openness and receptivity, the more we will assist it in happening.

What we do when we see the best in others is assist in drying up the psychic energies that wrap them in a cocoon of complacency and fear.

When we see all people in their best light, we coax them out of the knee-jerk position of primal mode.

In primal mode, people react without thought and are easily influenced. The way to keep them in primal mode is to keep introducing fear; fear of the enemy, fear of harm to their family, and fear of God.

When people are able to see their own empowerment, it is because they are not so readily gripped in fear. Hate and fear vibrate at similar frequencies. So, if you don't want people to change, hate them and demonize them.

Love dries up hate and fear. People in fear get stuck in the programming that they are given and are not able to discuss anything in regard to it. All they can do is repeat the talking points they were programmed with. Love dries up the psychic energy that keeps them from realizing their own abilities to discern.

If you want to assist humanity, see everyone as loving, competent, valuable, dynamic and worthy. This is in an abstract way that in no way condones their behavior. What needs to happen is an outpouring of unconditional love. What we are a part of, at the grassroots level of assisting humanity, is the shift from taking to giving.

The more you give your benevolence to others and focus on their good, the more you make space in the world for more goodness. Forgo making sweeping comments about the state of affairs on the surface. Water melts from underneath so the thin facade that seems intact is pierced last.

Kindness to all. It may sound like a Pollyanna point of view. But that is merely demonizing a powerful spiritual law. Love supersedes all else. Love dries up hate. Love dries up fear and Love reminds us all of our true nature. If you want to feel defeated, perpetuate hate. If you want to be empowered, be a powerhouse for Love.

THE POWER of Our Collective Love

The illusion of evil is predicated on need. Need creates pockets of stagnant energy that seem to take on a life of their own. It is really the imprinting of those who have contributed to the pockets of neglect. The persona we perceive in 'evil' is no more conscious than the involuntary actions of a snake whose head has been removed.

If one fixates on evil, they are merely feeding the pockets of stagnant energy and supplying the concept of evil as a permanent home. The fear of evil feeds evil. Just like the fear of dusting creates more dust. Those that act with malice and cruelty merely display their own deficiencies and need.

If you want to dry up evil in the world, validate those in need around you as much as possible. Assist those whom you are compelled to assist. Validate yourself and dry up all need from within. This is the most dynamic work you can do

We have all been trained to sacrifice ourselves. This creates desperation and a need to be fulfilled. This was the ploy of those who infiltrated our spiritual teachings and taught us to grow need at a systemic level. Unworthiness and false humility create need. Those who advance when individuals denounce their own importance are the takers. Please wake up from being had.

Instead of having perpetual pissing contests with anyone who compares, why not try the opposite? Why not work to validate and empower those around you? Some of the most validating healing work can come through simply the sincere practice of empowering others. In a way, it raises your vantage point to one who is capable of bestowing heartfelt benevolence on others.

The kindest thing you can do for anyone is to simply give them your attention. Satiate that longing in them to be heard and acknowledged. All of life will speak to you if you but listen to it. The most mind-numbing reality is that humans who are on autopilot will only acknowledge and value their own kind.

The most heinous act of cruelty I have ever witnessed happened this week. When supposedly important men went to visit the male immigrants who were locked up and did not even acknowledge them as human beings or their plight. They treated them like non-humans. This was intentional and overt. The malicious intention was to invalidate their humanity.

There are things within myself that I must do to reckon with holding space with such cruelty walking among us. Of course, I immediately send my energy to all the men, women and children who are in captivity and pour my love and encouragement onto them. I dissipate the psychic energy of trauma and fear that is being harvested from their plight and I send the energy back to them so they can remain whole.

I expand my consciousness so I can go to each one individually and reassure them that they are heard and are important. I use my love to encourage each one to stay strong and empowered and pull them off the time track so they can see how relatively temporary is their plight. I pour into them the message of their own importance.

I forgo more traditional prayers to invest all my intentions to drying up the need that is intentionally inflicted on the innocents. I spend my days and nights honing my abilities to dissipate the psychic energy of need and encouraging those who are set up to be needy. I practice pouring love into all the crevices of need in the world so that it becomes an automatic mechanism of my mind, heart and existence. It has become as habitual and regular as breathing.

The trick to being more effective is to keep your vantage point from afar. That way you can cover all the issues in the whole world and not just the ones that you are privy to. Someone who is devastated by one incident is keeping their vantage point too low to the ground to be as effective. It can also wreak havoc on one's nervous system and wear out the body too easily.

It is important to maintain balance when giving so much of yourself out so as to maintain longevity in your abilities to assist. A good hard cry once in a while is a great means of self-cleansing. It is also a way to align the different levels of your own consciousness, so you aren't overtaxing your physical, emotional or mental bodies too much and becoming numb in one or another.

Stretching beyond what your mind can fathom is the process of awakening, because the heart can expand ever so further than what the mind can endure. So, to stretch the intentions of the heart while maintaining a balanced mind is a noble and amazing feat. Doing so allows balance for others to do the same. This loving beyond the concepts of the mind is the most powerful contribution you can give to humanity.

Because the cruelty is so heinous these days, I find myself coping with the takers in a more hands-on approach. I found myself watching the desecration of human life and so desperately wanted to react. But my understanding of energy makes me realize that if I react in anger and outrage that I am automatically feeding the power-mongers who will use that energy as fuel, so I will myself to refrain.

Instead, I find myself visualizing scooping up all those who are inflicting suffering on others. I visualize a big fishing net. I scoop up the ones who are so hardwired and separate from the love. Then I treat them as if they are a huge net of hard-shelled crustaceans. The shell they carry is actually much harder. Then I visualize taking a huge mallet and pounding it down on them as a group as I lay the net on the ground. I pound and I pound to crush and break off their shells and reveal the soft underbelly of vulnerability in them.

There is something satisfying in crushing that shell on them. It is the shell that prevents them from feeling or even identifying with the suffering they are committing. I wish them no harm and no ill will. I merely assist in helping them be as vulnerable to the suffering of the collective as the most sensitive of humanity is.

Also, many people have come to the understanding of not feeding issues with their energy. It is good in one way, but it has led to an apathetic world. Without an understanding of our own potential and capabilities, we remove ourselves from the issues at hand but create a thick facade of apathy that all of humanity has to move through. That is what the inaction of not realizing our own empowerment has caused.

The awareness that I share assists to dry up the paralyzing apathy and allow individuals to reach beyond time and space, connect with others who are suffering and shift their whole reference points of reality by expanding their consciousness and fortitude simply through love.

Anyone who is reading this has the potential to alleviate the suffering on a grand scale. All they simply have to do is realize their own nature and capabilities and invest their energies to kindness through energetic validation. This is done through dropping the fixation on one's own perceived plight and direct their intentions onto assisting others. The Zen of doing this is that by focusing on others instead of yourself, it can dry up your own perceived plight more than most action.

As you read this, get a sense of all the others who are reading this as well. Know it is a miracle in itself that you are reading this. The multitudes have been convicted to death throughout history for sharing less truth than this.

As you read this, get a sense of the others who are reading this and automatically started to pour their love and kindness into the collective and each individual in the collective. Feel the synergy of our connection. Sense the passion and the purity of this intention.

This synergy of incredible Sacred Love acts like a bleaching agent to all those who strive to take and use cruelty as a weapon. It disarms them. Get a sense of them rendered ineffective. In tapping into the synergy of our effectiveness, we thwart the practices that have fed the takers of the world. Watch the behavior dry up like mold introduced to the light.

This could be our most important work on the planet thus far. This could be the reason we incarnated now. This is what all the power mongers of history have so desperately tried to prevent in us from realizing and achieving: the mere realization of the power of our collective love. Feed this love and the others reading this with the same fervor as yourself.

We are strong and empowered in all moments. We dissipate all 'evil' And we draw all souls everywhere into the love. This intention is my perpetual prayer.

EVAPORATE All Hate

The back and forth of 'them versus us' just feeds them. If you really want to dry up the hate in the world, you have to refrain from flinging your barbs and quips. There is an imbalanced faction in the world being fed by the hate monger in chief. They are stockpiling hate.

They cannot be met on their own terms. It is up to us who are aware to transcend the back and forth and dissipate the stockpile of psychic energy that is intended to fuel the head hate monger in chief's agenda.

(Say three times while tapping on your head and say it a fourth time while tapping on your chest.)

"We thwart the psychic practice of inciting violence by hate mongers; in all moments."

"We mute the voice of all hate mongers; in all moments."

"We hold all hate mongers to task; in all moments."

"We disarm all the hate mongers; in all moments."

"We dissipate all the psychic energy generated by the back and forth of them versus us; in all moments."

"We backwash the hate back onto the sender and render them helpless by their own intention; in all moments."

"We strip all hate mongers down to their vulnerabilities; in all moments."

"We eliminate the first cause of all hate mongers; in all moments."

"We close all portals to hate; in all moments."

"We dissipate all crazed intentions with the purity of our love; in all moments."

"We remove all engrams of civil war; in all moments."

"We close all portals to civil war; in all moments."

"We evaporate all hate; in all moments."

"We shift our paradigm from hate to love; in all moments."

EXPANSION OF HEAVEN

$\mathcal{O}$*utgrowing the Family Business*

If you were born into a family of bricklayers, there is a greater chance that you will grow up to be a bricklayer yourself. If you had two teachers for parents, it is more likely you would grow up to teach yourself. The same is true with any profession, be it public service, blue collar or business owner.

We learn our station in life from the conditions and ideology that we were born into. If it is a tight-knit family, it can be difficult to change professions because of all the expectations that are put on us. For the family to continue to be so tight and to relate, it is helpful if they share the same vantage point, speak the same vernacular, and share the same beliefs.

The same is true with society as a whole. You are a dynamic awakening spiritual being that is ready to experience enlightenment. But you are trapped in the family business of primal mode. It is primal mode because the majority members of the tribe think no differently than when they lived in trees and came walking out of the jungles.

Forcing others to suffer without concern of their plight is not a worthy position of the dynamic ones who are awakening. Being in agreement with the suffering in the world through your silence is not indicative of the spiritually awakened. Being afraid to express your true feelings because it will cause a negative rebuke is still living in the family business of primal mode.

Enjoying killing anything, even with the thin veneer of an excuse that it's food, is still enjoying killing. Thinking you are a member of a superior group that is more important than others is pure ignorance. Making a sport out of the suffering of any being is barbaric. Defending any political stance that advocates crimes against humanity with bravado is very much carrying on the family business of shortsighted tribalism. There is no longer any stomach for this as more and more of us awaken.

If you were able to talk honestly to your siblings in the family business, they would say that they really didn't want to follow in dad or mom's footsteps, but they didn't want to disappoint. Who are you trying not to disappoint by playing it small and allowing your great light to be squelched? Who do you serve?

Maybe it's an outmoded concept of a God that threatens you if you think outside the rule box. Maybe it is a conditioning that says that you live only one very short stint of existence and then waft off into the unknown. Maybe it is unseen forces that keep you immersed in fear and harnesses your unused potential for their own political gain. Maybe it is memories of all the times that you did try to speak up for yourself in past lives but were pulled out of the crowd, tortured, rebuked or abandoned.

In this limited society we are not allowed to acknowledge our past lives, let alone study the way they have formulated our present self. Everything we think, feel, understand and fear was formulated methodically into us by a force unlimited by the filters of a human brain or motivated by the musings of a human heart. In fact, the whole purpose of all that we have endured and suffered is to lead to one thing.

All that we have endured to this point is to give us every vantage point possible in life from beggar to king so that we can have compassion for every set of circumstances that exists. Our experiences are meant to stretch our capacity for compassion and awaken us to the plight of others in a very personal way. We are awakening our god senses to expand the consciousness of the whole. We are not separate from God. We wear Its cloth.

There is not a day when I do not cry at all the suffering that still exists. *How much do I have to write, how many taps do I have to post, how many assaults do I have to endure for all others to awaken their passion to the plight of the collective?* Anyone who says they are an empath is still misunderstanding what is really occurring. They are evolving past the limiting conditioning of their family business and experiencing what it is like to be tapped into the collective.

It is not enough to just feel others' pain and sit in a pool of martyrdom lamenting the pain that you feel. If you are tapped into the collective to feel their pain, you can send love, healing energy, encouragement and truth to all others through the same collective channels.

When I write, I am not just writing to the few people that the social media algorithm gods allow to see my posts. I am sending my love, passion and truth right into the heart of the collective, so those who may never hear of me will still benefit from my intention.

Instead of lamenting the humiliation, rejection and pain that you have endured in life, realize that it was intentional in a way to kick you out of the family business. You are too special to willingly coexist with those still trapped in primal mode. As a matter of fact, the pain and suffering that you have endured to expand your consciousness is as predictable and as formula as a mother bird kicking her baby out of the nest to teach it to fly.

You are on the precipice of flying. You are awakening. You no longer agree with the barbaric practices that have kept you ensconced in a limited reality, one that is so small that there is no room to move around in it. There is no way to share your gifts, speak your truth, or even love in a way that doesn't need defending. How much are we stooping to stay glued to such petty practices?

Unfurl your wings. Stop looking back into the nest by telling your sad tale. No one cares because they are obsessed with their own flight. Join in the wonder of awakening. As scary as it seems, break through the illusion of the power mongers and simply speak truth, show kindness and exercise compassion. It is not lost. It is never a waste. Every altruistic act is etched in the blueprint of the galaxies and expands our heavens.

The Tumbler Technique

You know those locks that are used on lockers? You open up the lock by lining up the three numbers and then the lock opens. You can use this visualization to change your mood at any time from depression to empowerment.

Whatever you are experiencing is a combination of three different choices that you are choosing to give life to. They are your experiences, feelings and thoughts. These three things are like the numbers you use to manifest any experience you are having.

Right now, most people are manifesting negative experiences by the three tumbler choices that they choose. They are dwelling on negative experiences, negative feelings and negative thoughts. This is sabotaging the human experience. You are capable of drawing upon any experience, feeling and thought. But by default, most people choose a triple whammy of negativity.

Try it. Check out what you are experiencing right now. Most likely, it has to do with lack, unworthiness, failure, illness, or a combination of any of those things. What is the negative experience that you are dwelling on? What is the thought process regarding the issue? What are the feelings regarding this issue? Pretty gloomy when you break it down, huh?

All you have to do is change the tumbler "numbers" that you are using to unlock a different reality. Instead of dwelling on the worst experience in the repertoire of your life, consciously choose an experience when you felt empowered. Instead of dwelling on a time when you felt defeated, focus on a time when you felt empowered.

Support this new experience that you are focusing on with positive thoughts and positive feelings. At first, your muscle memory is going to fight you and try to revert to the most negative experiences, thoughts, and feelings that come naturally. Fight this tendency every time you think of it.

UNIVERSAL SELF-REALIZATION

(Say three times while tapping on your head and say it a fourth time while tapping on your chest.)

"We make space in this world for all individuals to realize their empowerment; in all moments."

"We remove all blockages to all individuals realizing their empowerment; in all moments."

"We open all portals to all individuals realizing their empowerment; in all moments."

"We stretch our capacity for all individuals to realize their empowerment; in all moments."

"We are centered and empowered in all individuals realizing their empowerment; in all moments."

"We resonate, emanate, and are interconnected with all life in all individuals realizing their empowerment; in all moments."

With this technique, you can transform your life.

FREEDOM

On the Cusp of Awakening

We were born into unique times. Right now is the perfect time to be born. It is a precipice of a new era. It is a time when all individuals, one by one, forego the heavy programming and conditioning of the past eras and agree to connect to Source from within as opposed to an outer mandate shoved down our throat by ritual or repetition by well-meaning parents.

We have been and are still living in the Dark Ages if we don't awaken our own instincts and ability to discern when it comes to connecting to Source. We treat it as a foreign great sovereign in a foreign region that is inaccessible to us except through asking permission from a grand poobah of some sort.

You know if someone is still in the Dark Ages if they have to reference a book or someone else to back the truth that they are sharing; or if they are still concerned with how others are worshiping, who they love or their procreation habits; or if they are very afraid at the concept of death and still unsure about the very natural process of crossing.

You know that as a group we are still lingering in the Dark Ages when we believe that we are the superior race, when we still kill lasciviously, when we live compartmentalized with little concern of the suffering that takes place around us or when we still give our power to a group dynamic outside of our self. You know you are in the Dark Ages if you are still based on taking as opposed to giving.

Awakening is a means of shifting from the fairytale of a male God that is not to be questioned in fear of punishment. It is not keeping silent and avoiding sharing our greatness out of some sense of false humility. It is daring to show our dynamo in a way that has never been revealed by one in human skin. It is reconnecting to ourselves as a living, breathing aspect of nature where giving and receiving is as effortless as breathing.

Do you want to be awakened? Forgo that obligatory event that you were told you must attend. Or avoid a whole holiday if it behooves you. If something doesn't make your spirit zing, then forgo participating. You are not a backdrop to the musings of someone else. When you get that heaviness of heart in thinking of something, it is your innate wisdom telling you that it is not something you want to partake in. Stop going to events where you are not an honored guest. In going, you are agreeing to the treatment that you receive.

Do you want to be awakened? Quit living your life at the mercy of time. Compartmentalizing your day into little snippets of obligation again and again. For some things you must agree to a time, but when possible, leave things open ended so you can move more naturally around in the freedom of the moment.

When someone keeps a very tight schedule, they are nailing themselves right into time, again and again. It is as painless and as unnecessary as being nailed to a cross. When you are able to find yourself enjoying a moment, don't allow anyone to pull you out of it by talking about the past or pulling you into the future with worry or regret.

The obsession with money is a ploy to keep us trapped in time and space. It harbors the belief that it is the small self that determines what you receive. It is not. It is the Universe that has provided for you since beyond the convention of time. It has given you every experience you have needed to grow and expand your consciousness.

Wanting to accrue more is a means of wanting to store up resources in time and space because in time and space you feel disconnected to the flow of life. It is the living, breathing process of giving and receiving. You stop the process of giving out of fear of not receiving and lose sync with the natural process of living awakened. The fear nudges out the love, and the love is the fluidity of life.

In fact, those who live in the Dark Ages live in so much fear that they don't realize how much it encapsulates them. Fear of not having enough, fear of losing, fear of looking silly, fear of letting others down, and fear of dying all entail the same fear: Fear of the unknown. Why don't you know? Because knowing was programmed out of you.

Did you know that most things you fear are not future events that could happen, but past lives things that you have already experienced? Being disconnected from our past lives makes us living, breathing generators of fears.

If you knew you had already died in a fall, wouldn't it make sense that you would be afraid of heights in this life? If you knew you were going to slip out of your body at death and continue in a new body and would most likely come back in the same group you left, wouldn't that ease your concerns about dying?

If you could realize your dreams are a time you slip out of your body and visit those who had slipped out of their body for good, wouldn't you give your dreams more attention? If you really knew and had the conviction that you were going to continue on in life with the same people you love now, wouldn't that ease your angst?

If we could let go of a vengeful, petty, menacing God who commanded us to inflict pain on others and control them, then we would more easily transcend the Dark Ages. If we could relinquish a lot of the fear that comes up as future possibilities to avoid instead of past life memories that we forgot, we would dissipate the fear in ourselves and the world. Less fear, more love. It's that simple.

If we could dissipate a lot of the fear of the unknown and dying, it would jerk us out of the pettiness of primal mode and notice as a collective how much unnecessary pain we inflict on others. If we are so steeped in fear that we are causing children and families to suffer and die at the border simply for asking for assistance, we have definitely not come out of the Dark Ages.

Anyone who is watching what is playing out at the border with officials actually pouring out the water that Good Samaritans left in the desert cannot tell me that we are not still in the Dark Ages. Where is the outrage, where is the growth, where is the advancement in consciousness? Where is the love?

The more we get over ourselves and stop the petty grievances of attacking someone in social media or trying to one-up them, the more we can edge away from the Dark Ages. We have some dynamic individuals incarnating now who are here to give themselves to the world. They are working on changing the flow of life from taking to giving. Instead of attacking them, find a way to support them. Your loving intentions are a great donation.

Don't think for a second that you are not important and your thoughts are private. I can sense the purity or putridness in one's thoughts, deeds and life. That is a unique aspect of living awakened. The more you guard your own thoughts, deeds and intentions, the more you can help clean out the stagnant energy of the collective.

Because we are all connected, the love and truth I pour out goes into the collective and you receive it, even if you don't read my post. You receive my love and truth. It uplifts you and gives you space to realize your own depth. That is why people have such a reaction to me. The concentrated love goes into their personal pool and stirs up the stagnant energy to release. Some resent this and attribute it to me. But it is inevitable that we evolve now. Too many have chosen to awaken.

The joy of the awakening is that you choose. You are the one who is empowered. What you do, say, think and intend does matter. You can feed the multitudes with your love or you can be a part of the cesspool of old consciousness that needs to release so we can all be awakened.

SESSION WITH A SUICIDE Bomber

Hey Jen, I have a little question. What do you think recurrent low-grade fever could be? I've read your posts and thought maybe you had an explanation for this misery I've been dealing with for 20 years now. Thank you.

Do the energetic cleanse with each of these issues:

- Being overheated in a past life.
- Fever in a past life.
- Engrams of past life fevers.

Can the sessions you do be done in chat or other kind of writing or do they have to be done on the phone? English isn't my first language and even if my knowledge is good, I feel much more comfortable when I write; I perceive and understand written messages better. I need to read something to understand it properly.

Yes. We can do the session right here if you want. It would help to hear your voice so I can read your sound frequency. I can read your issues from your voice.

I will just say a few words in video. I want a session because I have been suffering from depression, anxiety, insomnia since my twenties in intervals. It grew into chronic fatigue and fibromyalgia. Also, get low-grade fever all the time. It's one of my biggest issues, this fever. Well, everything is an issue. I'm a difficult case. I also have post- traumatic stress syndrome because of traumatic childhood and war. God knows what more.

I will be on my computer later and we can set up a time. Maybe today.

It is better to do tomorrow so I can learn things from you. The healing has already started with you. You are already releasing. Not sure if you will be able to relax enough to feel it but it has started.

Are you ready for your session?

Yes.

Take a deep breath.

Each phrase I give you: Say each statement I give you three times slowly while continuously tapping on the top of your head. Then say the same statement a fourth time while tapping on your chest.

Got it.

"I release the trauma of war; in all moments."

"I release being the shock absorber of war; in all moments."

"I remove all the devastation that war has put in me; in all moments."

Ah...I see a past life issue.

"I release being covered in shrapnel; in all moments."

"I release dying in war; in all moments."

I see you almost as a suicide bomber.

I'm not surprised. I do punish myself the most.

We are very close to the trauma, and the pain in your body now is the shards of glass in your body. You were next to a storefront. That is why you are hesitant to cross in front of a glass window

"I release martyring myself for war; in all moments."

Immediately after you died, you realized how ridiculous it was to die but also how ridiculous the fighting was. You kind of hold to that now.

"I release reliving my death; in all moments."

"I release being coerced into a cause; in all moments."

"I release using pain as an excuse not to get involved; in all moments."

"I remove all the shrapnel in my causal body; in all moments."

"I remove all engrams of martyring myself; in all moments."

"I remove all engrams of blowing myself up; in all moments."

"I release being manipulated into blowing myself up; in all moments."

The group that talked you into doing it was your friends. You were coerced into doing it. You were stroked and loved thinking you were doing something noble.

"I remove the horrific sounds of war jamming my sound frequency; in all moments."

"I remove the horrific images jamming my light emanation; in all moments."

"I release micromanaging the universe; in all moments."

"I release holding onto the pain; in all moments."

"I release the belief I deserve the pain; in all moments."

"I release the belief that god is punishing me; in all moments."

"I release punishing myself; in all moments."

"I recant my vow of martyrdom; in all moments."

I am having a real hard time staying awake as I assist you energetically. If I stop typing, it means I passed out and will get back to you when I come to.

Oh, ok. But why?

Because I am working with you at a very deep level, deeper than the conscious mind can reach.

"I recant all vows and agreements between myself and war; in all moments."

"I recant my vow of servitude; in all moments."

"I release being very stubborn; in all moments."

"I release being rigid; in all moments."

"I release keeping pain as a memento; in all moments."

"I recant all vows of self-deprivation; in all moments."

"I recant my vow of solitude; in all moments."

"I release hiding the fear with bravado; in all moments."

"I release jumping off a bridge; in all moments."

Are you felling any relaxation in your body?

Feeling little tired.

I am very tired. LOL. I cannot stay awake.

You need a break?

No, I know what I do. You are the one who does not know. Can you take a nap now? I can work on you inwardly and we can come back to the surface stuff at another scheduled time. I want to give you a bunch of taps to do the energetic cleanse with.

When I get so sleepy, it is to assist energetically. Can you sleep now?

I think I could.

Good. This has happened before. Sometime today I will post a bunch of things for you to do the energetic cleanse on. And we can connect tomorrow at the same time as today.

I got some really hard anxiety when we stopped, still having it.

You are releasing. Try to relax into it. The energy is being pulled out, but you are identifying with it, so you feel like something bad is happening. Do this tap: "I release identifying with the pain and trauma; in all moments."

In fact, do the energetic cleanse with:

Identifying with the pain and trauma.

Then do the energetic cleanse with the ego.

I will give you more topics to do the energetic cleanse with. You are fine. I am glad you are having a reaction. It is evidence that there is a shift.

Just give me one for this fever I've been having for weeks. I'm literally going crazy.

Being burned alive.

Oh, wow.

Yes, you are trapped in the explosion. Do taps on:

The explosion, war, being martyred, the bombing, shards of glass, being shredded.

Do all these with the energetic cleanse exercise one by one.

It's a lot. Ok, getting on it now, starting with burned alive. I feel it working.

I connected to you in my dreams too.

Yes, that is why we had to sleep. I was helping you.

My anxiety stopped after tapping last night!

Okay good.

I worked all morning and was so excited.

Do more taps: Suicide, desecrating your life, feverish agitation, control, all old oaths and vows.

Okay, the whole energetic cleanse?

Absolutely! You don't have to do them so quickly. Do them at a more relaxed pace. Others can't help you by the way. They do not work at the level that we do, and you don't need more energy via prayers. You need stagnant energy released.

Let me know when you are done. You know you killed yourself in a past life. That causes incredible pain to the person who that happens to. You are working through that desecration of your own spirit. That is why it has been so difficult for you.

Desecrating my life was hard.

Do: killing yourself, indifference to life, killing others, committing genocide.

CLEAR YOUR BRAIN *Fog*

The whole concept of a smoking gun is nailing in the misnomer that we can't think for ourselves; that we must have all the details of an intention laid at our feet until we can act. We are being paralyzed into inaction by this concept.

What is playing out in society at large is also playing out in our own personal lives. These taps will assist us all. They will also assist all of humanity to accept the truth of the actions that are playing out.

The world is desperate for us to assist them in awakening.

Freedom

(Say three times while tapping on your head and say them a fourth times while tapping on your chest.)

"I declare myself a surrogate for humanity in doing these taps; in all moments."

"I release the disconnect between cause and effect; in all moments."

"I release disregarding the effects of obvious causes; in all moments."

"I release filtering out the effect of obvious causes; in all moments."

"I release the need to be bombarded by a series of effects to validate the initial cause; in all moments."

"I recognize the effect as readily as I acknowledge the cause; in all moments."

"I strengthen the synapses between cause and effect; in all moments."

"I dissipate all psychic energy that prevents me from acknowledging the effects of all causes; in all moments."

"I strip away all illusions that hide the effects of all causes; in all moments."

"I dissipate the psychic energy that highlights alternative facts as reality; in all moments."

"I release being hypnotized or manipulated into believing in alternative facts; in all moments."

"I am impervious to being programmed by repetition; in all moments."

"I release ascribing outer sources as a source for truth; in all moments."

"I release believing outer sources over my own compass; in all moments."

"I release deferring to an outer agenda; in all moments."

"I release being immersed in apathy by refusing to acknowledge truth; in all moments."

"I release the fear of acknowledging all the effects of all causes; in all moments."

"I release being deduced to a mental stupor; in all moments."

"I release being paralyzed in inaction; in all moments."

"I release the fear of being wrong; in all moments."

"I release being ostracized for speaking truth; in all moments."

"I release being tortured or killed for speaking truth; in all moments."

"I release the need to be polite in refusing to address an initial wrong; in all moments."

"I release doubting myself; in all moments."

"I release turning my integrity into mush; in all moments."

"I release confusing strength for anger; in all moments."

"I access my strength without engaging in anger; in all moments."

"I release burying my truth and causing disease; in all moments."

"I maintain my outer calm without dipping into apathy; in all moments."

"I eliminate the first cause in the disconnect between each cause and each effect; in all moments."

"I strengthen the conviction in acknowledging the effect of each cause; in all moments."

"I release being so easily conditioned; in all moments."

"I shift my paradigm from being conditioned to knowing truth; in all moments."

"I embrace the randomity of truth; in all moments."

"I hard wire the true effects to all causes; in all moments."

"I trust my ability to discern truth; in all moments."

"I scrutinize all outer facts and sources against the master truth of my own inner compass; in all moments."

"I am centered and empowered and confidently discerning truth; in all moments."

"I release being closed off to truth; in all moments."

"I stay perpetually open to realizing more truth; in all moments."

"I disregard all lies that I accepted as truth; in all moments."

"I undo the programming and conditioning of all lies; in all moments."

"I resonate, emanate and am interconnected with all life in confidently discerning truth; in all moments."

"I am a portal of truth; in all moments."

"All lies dissipate in my wake; in all moments."

"I am awakened; in all moments."

THE ISSUE of Abortion

(Say each statement three times while tapping on your head and say it a fourth time while tapping on your chest.)

"We dissipate the psychic streams of energy that deem to control women through the abortion issue; in all moments."

"We strip the illusion off of all factions that tempt to enslave humanity through the abortion issue; in all moments."

"We remove the negative charge from the word abortion; in all moments."

"We remove the negative charge from the word socialism; in all moments."

"We release confusing socialism for communism; in all moments."

"We release the attack of freedom by demonizing the issue of abortion; in all moments."

"We dissipate the psychic streams of energy that control the masses hiding behind the abortion issue; in all moments."

"We dissipate the psychic streams of energy that hide behind religion to control the masses; in all moments."

"We dissipate the psychic streams of energy that flood mass media and social media to control the narrative; in all moments."

"We release the psychic streams of energy that work to divide the masses and pit them against each other; in all moments."

"We dissipate the psychic streams of energy that strive to prevent humanity from awakening; in all moments."

"We dissipate the psychic streams of energy that bury truth; in all moments."

"We dissipate the psychic streams of energy that demonize those who strive to uplift humanity; in all moments."

"We dissipate the psychic streams of energy of religious control; in all moments."

"We dissipate the psychic streams of energy of a one-life narrative; in all moments."

TAKING Selfies

The Native Americans didn't believe in allowing their picture to be taken. It was a form of capturing the essence of a person and trapping them. In a way it is because the subjects of the pictures are going to be trapped in the experience of the image. At least an aspect of them is.

Why do you think it is so easy to take photos these days? It is a means of trapping an aspect of individuals in the experience and preventing them from transcending. That is why it is such a disservice to take pictures of someone in a hospital. They are being seen at their worst. It traps them in the pain of that experience. That is how they are being seen by others.

If you don't like images of yourself, maybe it isn't a self-loathing thing but a deeper understanding of the dynamics in play when allowing your image to be taken. Do you really want to be seen forever with your arm around someone who you are trying to free yourself from karmically? Perhaps your innate wisdom has a better sense than the conscious you.

(Say each statement three times while tapping on your head and say it a fourth time while tapping on your chest.)

"I free my energy from all pictures of me; in all moments."

"I free all of humanity from being trapped in pictures; in all moments."

"I dissolve all engrams of suffering; in all moments."

"I dissolve all engrams that prevent the awakening of humanity; in all moments."

"I free all souls galvanized in the imagery of suffering; in all moments."

"I free humanity from being galvanized in the imagery of suffering; in all moments."

"I free up all of my joy, love, abundance, freedom and wholeness to be self-realized; in all moments."

"I free up all of humanity's joy, love, abundance, freedom and wholeness to be self-realized; in all moments."

"I am centered and empowered in being free of any limiting viewpoints of me; in all moments."

"Humanity is centered and empowered in being free of all limiting viewpoints of it; in all moments."

Transcendence

The way religions fail people is by holding them hostage to the illusion of goodness. It is impossible to be good all the time and to be balanced. Since balance entails equal amounts of all experiences, balance means balancing all positive issues and traits within one's self as a means to transcend.

If one only acknowledges the good in themselves, they allow the negativity to fester within them when it has no attention on it. This is when you see good people get corrupted. They are too busy mandating goodness in all, that they allow the negativity in themselves to become unmanageable.

It may be acerbated when one is in a position to have a say in how others conduct themselves. Their attention on others further prevents them from seeing the demons they allow to fester in their own energy system. We see this in society now.

(Say each statement three times while tapping on your head and say it a fourth time while tapping on your chest.)

"I release the need to be good; in all moments."

"I release the need to be seen; in all moments."

"I release the need to be perfect; in all moments."

"I release the need to advance beyond my brethren; in all moments."

"I release the need to be right; in all moments."

"I release the need to be helpful; in all moments."

"I release the need to excel; in all moments."

HEALING

⬥

U **nder Energetic Attack**
    Social media is actually a gift to humanity to give them a
chance to awaken. We are all connected through this dynamic venue. But it is
also being used to try to more thoroughly enslave humanity.

I don't usually discuss issues of health and assault. I understand the dynamics of the interplay between the illusion that we are here and the reality that plays out beyond the illusion. Many of you know I have had a rough life. To me, that is just formula for bringing truth to the masses. Others have tried and their messages have been warped.

Many know my story. I was imprisoned by someone who was wrapped up in conspiracy theories, starved and forced to work under incredible conditions and went through the process of enlightenment. It is a formula experience. Instead of working to be good, you face all your demons until you realize that it is all an illusion and you transcend all the aberrations that the ego creates.

I came back to this reality eleven years ago thinking I was a retarded boy. No therapist could relate. Family rejected me and friends dispersed. My only saving grace was the connection to my Guides and their propping me up to help others. I did not realize how important my work is to assisting others in understanding their own empowerment.

What I do and what I have endured is incredible. I look around at my life and it is all consuming in assisting humanity. Petty distractions of loved ones and social events are non-existent. I have been consumed by the work I share, specifically in realizing its importance.

Recently, I have been under more of an energetic attack than the usual barrage. In this physical illusion, it is people chastising my work and telling me that what I am doing is wrong. Yet I can see their limitations. They clearly do not see the scope of what I do. They are still in the grip of male dominance. Yet they want me gone.

The healers that I use for my own advisement have seen the assault that I am under. They have tapped into what I have known and try to convey to people who get my work, that they need to step up into their empowerment. But when I tell people that, they think it is me asking them something for myself. I can assure you that it is not.

In fact, the more that I am seen in the world, the more difficult it becomes. The world is not used to selfless beings and attributes my work to what they have experienced here, which is being duped, raped and stolen from. They are afraid to step up in their own empowerment because they attribute it to sacrifice and pain.

I assure you that my life has been this. I am like the lead duck that breaks the resistance so that all other ducks can glide through the resistance. But all the ducks are afraid to even fly in formation. They are afraid to step up to their empowerment.

My healer-adviser tapped into the resistance of most people in fulfilling their soul contract. They are terrified of what they have agreed to do. Yet they are restless here in the world of mass enslavement, and more and more frustrated at their inability to affect change. But they can. It doesn't need to be a scary process. If you are feeling like your life lacks meaning, you may want to do these taps.

Please see the Energetic Cleanse from Chapter 13 and do the exercise with this phrase:

"Fear of stepping up to fulfilling my soul contract"

You may want to even do it as a surrogate for humanity. You do that by starting the exercise with this tap:

"I declare myself a surrogate for humanity in doing these taps; in all moments."

You may think by doing this, you are making more of a commitment. But there are factions that do not want you to know how empowered you are. They use everything you know and believe to prevent your awakening. If your present belief system were working for you, you would not feel helpless in any way.

If I have helped you in any way and you are grateful for the freedom it has brought, please do these taps.

Find them on my website also: www.jenuinehealing.com/energetic-cleanse-sign-up-form/

THE EIGHTH SENSE

I was asking myself a question in the way that I do to get answers. I was contemplating on how easy life is to perceive in energy because then you are not so easily duped by others. For example, when you aren't taking everything at face value, meaning you are delving beneath the shiny facade of circumstance, you can see the real dynamics that are at play.

People will not be able to lie so easily. You will see the distortion in their energy as they do. People will still try to lie to themselves, but you will be able to see the distortion in that as well. Perceiving in energy brings clarity to every situation. One may have blind spots for themselves but will be more clear to assess the situation at hand.

An example of this is a mother who seems to have superpowers in knowing her children's behavior. She is tapped into every nuance of their life because she is so vested in her love for them and what is best for them. She is using all she knows about her children, all the dynamics she has observed in them, and her own instincts for what is best for them.

The mother's instinct is the closest thing to understand the eighth sense. Imagine if the mother could not only have a heightened sense of awareness with her children but also all of life. This is achievable. In fact, it is very freeing. This is actually a great way to explain the vantage point that I hold.

When contemplating this information, I asked myself what about the sixth sense and seventh sense? I am always amazed that I receive the answers to any question I ask. I was shown how the sixth sense is perceiving astral nuances like animals do. This ability is accessible to humans as well if they only would allow themselves to believe.

The sixth sense is also all the abilities to connect with those who have crossed. Those who have crossed have merely slipped out of their physical body and continue to exist in a vibration that is more subtle than the coarse physical existence. Since the body they are in matches the vibration of the realm they are in, their world is as solid as it was on the physical realm.

Since an aspect of ourselves is astral, it is easy to slip into our astral perceptions if we have an understanding of them. In fact, people do, and don't understand what is happening. When someone wakes up and is paralyzed from moving, they are actually still in their astral body and operating from the astral realm and don't realize it because the astral plane is so close to the physical plane.

The seventh sense is being able to read the Akashic records of others without much effort. All wounds, shames, and fears are a reflection of past life trauma. When I look at someone, I can see all the past lives that overlay and affect their present life.

If I am able to perceive peoples' past lives, others are capable as well. But the social conditioning that "we only live one life," drastically reduces this ability. Since over eighty percent of what is irrelevant is filtered out of the human brain, filtering out the acceptance of reincarnation also filters out the ability to perceive past lives. This holds true with other subtle perceptions as well.

If one believes that they are ostracized to a remote intangible place after they die, of course their brain is going to filter out all connections with loved ones that cross over. But those who believe in the connection between realms will get a "sense" of their loved ones around.

They will even get messages from the other side. They are able to stay connected to those who have crossed. They may even remember that they visit their loved ones in the dream state and merely forget when they awake. This happens all the time, but the human brain filters out such visits.

The eighth sense is a compilation of being totally plugged into the present moment in life and not filtering out the important nuances. It is about scrutinizing every thought, deed, and feeling to know where it is originating from and whether it is about you or just energy you are walking into.

The eighth sense also incorporates all the subtle cues of the sixth sense and being able to see the past life influences as a dynamic. It is being so far above the curve of what others perceive because you have deemed it important and relevant. You care about all expressions of life and the quality of experiences for all.

It is like you walk on energetic rice paper to not leave anyone or anything worse for the wear for knowing you. You are kind to a fault and still aware of all the subtle nuances where you can do better. In caring so much for the spiritual dynamics of all, you tap into direct knowing.

It seems that you know anything you ask of the Universe. There is no need to store information in the brain. The Universe exchanges truth with you willingly and happily. You have made space in your world for truth and kindness and the Universe responds in kind. This is the eighth sense.

This Is What I Do

I was talking to a friend who was feeling lonely. She may not have felt it, but I felt this horrific pain and isolation in her as we were talking about the nonsense of the day.

I felt it in her abdominal cavity. When I pointed it out, she felt it too. What I did was isolate it and separate it from her so she could recognize it and separate it from herself. I asked if I could clear it. She agreed.

It felt all stringy and attached to her like the guts of a pumpkin. She has done a lot of my taps that I put out, so she was used to the energetic shifts. This felt like the last deluge of some kind. It felt like this cave of horrific experiences I encountered within before I passed through enlightenment. But this was hers.

I tapped into a past life of hers. She was in a chicken body. She was a watcher even way back then. She watched the other chickens get slaughtered by having their heads chopped off. They squawked and they clucked, and they sounded ridiculous. No one was going to save them she thought. She just numbly watched as her friends were arbitrarily slaughtered.

I asked my friend if she felt that tightness in the left side of her neck. I isolated that pain so she could differentiate it from the rest of her. She felt it. I told her that that was where the cleaver struck down on her and chopped her head off in one hearty swing.

It was her turn. There was no mercy for her. No compassion. She chose not to squawk like the other chickens. She left her eyes open and just stared obliquely. That is the pain and horror she had stored in the present body. She didn't complain or try to get anyone to help. She was resolved that there was nothing to do but get through the experience and perish. She did not want to carry on like the others.

I cried her pain for a few minutes. It was the deep buried anguish of her chicken body that stored itself in her present-day neck. It was stagnant energy that I released. I squawked and carried on like she could have done way back when she was killed for her body's meat. I made as much fuss as was necessary to validate her pain and to actually dissipate it.

I sat with the chicken in an altered state as the cleaver fell down and severed the head. I stayed present with the chicken and assisted it in being aware of crossing over on the other side. The chicken was trapped in the moment of horror realizing it still existed, but so close to the experience that it still identified with the body and felt the horror of being headless.

I sat with the chicken experience and watched as the chicken snapped out of the trauma. It suddenly opened its eyes and realized it was whole. It was calm on the other side. The chicken flapped its wings and wandered off. The pain in the neck subsided.

I visualized scooping the stringy energy out of the abdomen and into a pile of loose energy as if her abdomen was a cave and the loose energy was at the mouth of the cave. A cleansing wind came along and whisked all the energy away. It dissipated in the wind.

My friend was then very tired as she felt these old sheaths of energy leave through her feet. Parts of her body that were locked up were now free. She released tension that she wasn't aware she had.

She no longer identified with the chicken that was at the mercy of life. I validated the chicken and her in the process. She did not have to suffer that incredible indignity and trauma ever again. She was validated at a very deep level. She is now more free.

THE PROFOUND REALIZATION and the Cure

I research all the ways that dis-ease is introduced into the body. It can be past lives, genetic propensities, or programming and conditioning from the past. There are emotional factors, belief systems, psychic influences, environmental imbalances and societal norms.

I have addressed them all in creating sets of taps for humanity to return to balance. It is great to see when people who do the taps become empowered. But it is also frustrating to know that there is so much that is still being missed.

I was talking to a very aware person who has benefited from my assistance. As I was watching him, I was seeing the places in him that still needed to be aligned better. As I was listening to him, the Akashic records of his conception opened up.

I saw his father's issues of insecurity, male bravado and frustration with being trapped in a nine to five play out. When he was thrusting the sperm into his wife to meet the egg, all these unwelcome issues were thrust out of him during the sex act. The sex act was a great release. But the issues accompanied the sperm when it met the egg.

All the issues of insecurity, male bravado and frustration fused into the merging of the egg and sperm as well. So, as the zygote of the baby's perfect beginning was being initiated, the issues of male bravado, insecurity and frustration were being duplicated into every cell of this new living person.

It is difficult to see how to address our own issues if they are stamped into every cell of our physical makeup. I myself am the product of two drunk, middle-aged people trapped in a desperate cycle of poverty and hopelessness, loathing the thought of having one more child on top of the nine they already couldn't cope with. I have seen these issues of hopelessness and unworthiness reflected in myself.

Imagine the issues of your parents. If you are able, ask a relative of their age what were the issues that they dealt with. Get a sense of how the issues could have gotten passed into you through the exchange of the sex act at your conception. Make a list of them and do them as a set of taps similar to the ones below. The possibilities are endless as a means to free yourself of the issues.

(Say each statement three times while tapping on your head and say it a fourth time while tapping on your chest.)

"I extract all hopelessness from my zygote; in all moments."

"I extract all poverty from my zygote; in all moments."

"I extract all frustration from my zygote; in all moments."

"I extract all fear from my zygote; in all moments."

"I extract all ignorance from my zygote; in all moments."

"I extract all depression from my zygote; in all moments."

"I extract all unworthiness from my zygote; in all moments."

"I extract all sadness from my zygote; in all moments."

"I extract all programing and conditioning from my zygote; in all moments."

"I extract all dis-ease from my zygote; in all moments."

"I extract all failure from my zygote; in all moments."

"I extract all slavery from my zygote; in all moments."

"I extract all insecurity from my zygote; in all moments."

"I extract all rejection from my zygote; in all moments."

"I extract all abandonment from my zygote; in all moments."

"I extract all conformity from my zygote; in all moments."

"I extract all chaos from my zygote; in all moments."
"I extract all schisms from my zygote; in all moments."
"I extract all judgment from my zygote; in all moments."
"I extract all ugliness from my zygote; in all moments."
"I extract all darkness from my zygote; in all moments."
"I extract all dysfunction from my zygote; in all moments."
"I extract all addictions from my zygote; in all moments."

THE ARMPIT of God

The angst you are feeling is not your own. You are tapping into the collective. What you feel is not meant for you to identify with but to allow it to pass through your body.

I think of us all as pores on the body of God. Pores are the body's way to release toxins from the body through sweating them out. Some pores release toxins more than others

People who are sensitive and struggling, I see them as the armpit of God. They are more capable of passing incredible angst out of the collective through their willing body. The more that we are all able to allow issues to pass through us without hanging on to them, the easier the release of such angst will be on everyone.

Right now, humanity is still struggling to make everyone aware how self-sabotaging it is to inflict pain on others. It only burdens us all. Thank you for what you pass through. Try to be grateful for your level of feeling. It is the upgrade to the indifference that is still being broken up on the planet. Thank you.

IMPROVE Your Eyesight

(Say each statement three times while tapping on your head and say it a fourth time while tapping on your chest.)
"I release seeing sadness everywhere; in all moments."
"I release seeing hate everywhere; in all moments."
"I release seeing poverty everywhere; in all moments."
"I release seeing slavery everywhere; in all moments."

"I release seeing disease everywhere; in all moments."

"I release seeing failure everywhere; in all moments."

"I release seeing danger everywhere; in all moments."

"I release seeing abandonment and rejection everywhere; in all moments."

"I release seeing conformity everywhere; in all moments."

"I release seeing war everywhere; in all moments."

"I release seeing death everywhere; in all moments."

"I release seeing fragmentation everywhere; in all moments."

"I release seeing ugliness everywhere; in all moments."

"I release seeing apathy and indifference everywhere; in all moments."

"I release seeing discontent everywhere; in all moments."

"I release seeing ignorance everywhere; in all moments."

"I release seeing tribalism everywhere; in all moments."

"I release seeing fear everywhere; in all moments."

"I release seeing weakness everywhere; in all moments."

"I release seeing cruelty everywhere; in all moments."

"I see Joy everywhere; in all moments."

"I see Love everywhere; in all moments."

"I see Abundance everywhere; in all moments."

"I see Freedom everywhere; in all moments."

"I see Health everywhere; in all moments."

"I see Success everywhere; in all moments."

"I see Safety everywhere; in all moments."

"I see Friendship everywhere; in all moments."

"I see Creativity everywhere; in all moments."

"I see Peace everywhere; in all moments."

"I see Life everywhere; in all moments."

"I see Wholeness everywhere; in all moments."

"I see Beauty everywhere; in all moments."

"I see Enthusiasm everywhere; in all moments."

"I see Contentment everywhere; in all moments."

"I see Spirituality everywhere; in all moments."

"I see Enlightenment everywhere, in all moments."

"I see Confidence everywhere; in all moments."
"I see Strength everywhere; in all moments."
"I see Compassion and Kindness everywhere; in all moments."
"I see Integrity and Truth everywhere; in all moments."
"I see Sincerity everywhere; in all moments."

IMPROVE *Your Hearing*

(Say each statement three times while tapping on your head and say it a fourth time while tapping on your chest.)

"I release hearing sadness everywhere; in all moments."
"I release hearing hate everywhere; in all moments."
"I release hearing poverty everywhere; in all moments."
"I release hearing slavery everywhere; in all moments."
"I release hearing disease everywhere; in all moments."
"I release hearing failure everywhere; in all moments."
"I release hearing danger everywhere; in all moments."
"I release hearing abandonment and rejection everywhere; in all moments."
"I release hearing conformity everywhere; in all moments."
"I release hearing war everywhere; in all moments."
"I release hearing death everywhere; in all moments."
"I release hearing fragmentation everywhere; in all moments."
"I release hearing ugliness everywhere; in all moments."
"I release hearing apathy and indifference everywhere; in all moments."
"I release hearing discontent everywhere; in all moments."
"I release hearing ignorance everywhere; in all moments."
"I release hearing tribalism everywhere; in all moments."
"I release hearing fear everywhere; in all moments."
"I release hearing weakness everywhere; in all moments."
"I release hearing cruelty everywhere; in all moments."
"I hear Joy everywhere; in all moments."
"I hear Love everywhere; in all moments."
"I hear Abundance everywhere; in all moments."

"I hear Freedom everywhere; in all moments."
"I hear Health everywhere; in all moments."
"I hear Success everywhere; in all moments."
"I hear Safety everywhere; in all moments."
"I hear Friendship everywhere; in all moments."
"I hear Creativity everywhere; in all moments."
"I hear Peace everywhere; in all moments."
"I hear Life everywhere; in all moments."
"I hear Wholeness everywhere; in all moments."
"I hear Beauty everywhere; in all moments."
"I hear Enthusiasm everywhere; in all moments."
"I hear Contentment everywhere; in all moments."
"I hear Spirituality everywhere; in all moments."
"I hear Enlightenment everywhere; in all moments."
"I hear Confidence everywhere; in all moments."
"I hear Strength everywhere; in all moments."
"I hear Compassion and Kindness everywhere; in all moments."
"I hear Integrity and Truth everywhere; in all moments."
"I hear Sincerity everywhere; in all moments."

ELIMINATE DEEP FAT

I asked the Universe how to regulate weight without diet or exercise. I received information to formulate these taps. Some people who have done them have felt an immediate shift.

Do these taps and mark this day. If you do these taps and start feeling more fit and alive, please trace it back to doing these taps. (Please do not do these taps if you are underweight.)

(Say three times while tapping on your head and say it a fourth time while tapping on your chest.)

"I activate the cellular switch to burn the deep fat in my body; in all moments."

"I turn on the master metabolism switch in my body; in all moments."

"I shrink all my fat cells down to prepubescent size; in all moments."

"I activate the AMPK enzymes in my body; in all moments."

"I activate the longevity enzymes in my body; in all moments."

"I thwart the nutritional overload of my cells; in all moments."

"I introduce the vibration of berberine to my fat cells; in all moments."

"I introduce the vibration of gynostemma to my fat cells; in all moments."

"I introduce the vibration of quercetin to my fat cells; in all moments."

"I eliminate the deep fat in my body; in all moments."

REPLENISH *Your Chi*

(Say each statement three times while tapping on your head and say it a fourth time while tapping on your chest.)

"I replenish my kidney Chi; in all moments."

"I replenish my liver Chi; in all moments."

"I replenish my pancreas Chi; in all moments."

"I replenish my heart Chi; in all moments."

"I replenish my intestinal Chi; in all moments."

"I replenish my endocrine Chi; in all moments."

"I replenish my emotional Chi; in all moments."

"I replenish my sexual Chi; in all moments."

"I replenish my vascular Chi; in all moments."

"I replenish my brain Chi; in all moments."

"I replenish my abundance Chi; in all moments."

"I replenish my stomach Chi; in all moments."

"I replenish my skeletal Chi; in all moments."

"I replenish my muscular Chi; in all moments."

"I replenish my nervous system Chi; in all moments."

"I replenish my skin Chi; in all moments."

"I replenish my cellular Chi; in all moments."

"I replenish my digestive Chi; in all moments."

"I replenish my happiness Chi; in all moments."
"I replenish my wellness Chi; in all moments."
"I replenish my enthusiasm Chi; in all moments."
"I replenish my spirituality Chi; in all moments."
"I replenish my kundalini Chi; in all moments."
"I replenish my dantien Chi; in all moments."
"I replenish my sensory Chi; in all moments."
"I replenish my ocular Chi; in all moments."
"I replenish my flexibility Chi; in all moments."
"I replenish the Chi of my meridians; in all moments."
"I replenish the Chi of my chakra system; in all moments."
"I replenish my creativity Chi; in all moments."
"I replenish my productivity Chi; in all moments."
"I replenish the Chi of my self-worth; in all moments."
"I replenish the Chi of my intuition; in all moments."
"I replenish the Chi of my self-love; in all moments."
"I replenish my compassion Chi; in all moments."
"I replenish the Chi of my truth; in all moments."
"I replenish my ability to awaken Chi; in all moments."
"I replenish my empowerment Chi; in all moments."

PSYCHIC DIVERSION

Last night, I woke up in the middle of the night with a health issue. Of course, I immediately knew what it was. The taps we have been doing are very effective. Protests are rising. Nuclear experiments are failing. The power mongers who are savvy to psychic control are getting thwarted using subtle tactics. They are concerned.

Scares about health are psychic means to stop an assault, by introverting those who are empowered. That is what concerns about health are. It is no accident that all commercials and airwaves are inundated with medicines and sick people telling their story. Don't fall for it.

There are things to do to address health issues, but don't be recoiled in fear. Don't obsess and don't be distracted from what is happening in the world because of it. Distraction is a great psychic ploy and it is infuriating to watch all the news outlets play such a part in the distraction, even when they are trying to be on point.

After I realized the undercurrent of what was going on, I went to sleep. In the dream state I was in an American shop that was overtaken by foreign influence. It was empty and was being cleared out. There were no clients. But that seemed fine to them. At one point, the president showed up as the bumbling idiot.

The shop was our government. It was gutted and a hollow shell, already taken over by the enemy. They were merely waiting until people got used to the shift before they moved more people in and took over management.

In the dream, there were all these clothes. There were very rich clothes and piles and piles of average clothes. They represented the lives they have overtaken through subversive means. The first daughter was trying on clothes of the rich. She was trying out the role of an oligarch. A ruling class princess.

There were so many of us working there who were aware but in over our heads. We tried to resist in subtle ways but did not know what to do. This dream is pretty much the state of affairs. The taps that I post are a very profound way to affectively dissipate the psychic currents of control and fear. They work.

We just can't get distracted into retreating. The tactic being used is health fears. Don't fall for it. Don't own any issue that comes to you. Just let it pass through. Address it physically without fixating on it or creating a subtext of drama around it.

(Say each statement three times while tapping on your head and say it a fourth time while tapping on your chest.)

"I dissipate all psychic energy regarding health scares; in all moments."

"I release falling for health scares; in all moments."

"I release recoiling in fear for any reason; in all moments."

"I maintain my empowerment and awareness in all moments."

"We dissipate all psychic streams of energy using health issues to distract; in all moments."

"We dissipate all psychic streams of energy intended to paralyze us in fear; in all moments."

"We thwart all attempts to kill democracy; in all moments."

"We thwart all attempts to throw the world into a fearful submissive state; in all moments."

"We immediately hold all key aggressors to stealing personal freedom accountable; in all moments."

"We immediately disarm all aggressors to personal freedoms; in all moments."

"We remove all masks, walls, armor, protection and support from all aggressors to personal freedoms; in all moments."

"We put a bubble of protection around all advocates of personal freedom including all speakers of truth, potential new leaders and every single protestor; in all moments."

"We immediately stop the practice of harvesting energy through scapegoating the innocent; in all moments."

"We thrust back on the aggressors their own intentions in harming others; in all moments."

"We awaken all those who are immersed in a psychic grip and assist them in freeing themselves; in all moments."

"We empower all those who see with the clarity and depth to thwart the psychic forces that desperately work to control us; in all moments."

"We stop the psychic practice of demonizing those who love and speak truth; in all moments."

"We stop the psychic practice of distractions through health issues, personalized victimization and attacking each other; in all moments."

"We dissipate all psychic streams of diversion; in all moments."

"We shift the universal currents to joy, love, abundance, health and freedom; in all moments."

"We free and awaken mass consciousness; in all moments."

After you break through the resistance and do these taps, feel the inner relief and freedom. Watch how they play out in the world. You are loved, appreciated and respected for taking the time to do them.

. . .

Combating *the Baconator*

There is a moral debate about whether eating meat is ethical. It does seem like such a personal issue for some. A more disturbing trend is associating eating meat with one's masculinity. It is done in advertisements that challenge people to eat as much meat as possible to show their voracity.

It is a means of triggering primal urges in the brain to sell more fast food. It is egregious. Because, when the brain is in primal mode, it loses its ability to discern. This is also done with blind patriotism, gun rights and heated political issues. There is no concern for the outcome or welfare of others, not while in primal mode. The more the individual can stay cornered in primal mode, the more they will react with the fervor of survival.

Advertisement is a trillion-dollar industry. The whole purpose is to have the product that is being sold associated with issues that the audience is passionate about. It then transfers the passion onto the product. This is done over and over again in every variable of ways.

That is why people aren't as free as they believe themselves to be. They are merely a compilation of the multitude of agendas that are flooded into their psyche on a given day. That is how the people with the most money are able to control the narrative of society. They have the most means of flooding the airwaves with their point of view.

That is what we are seeing play out in society today. One side is more susceptible to the agendas being pumped into the airwaves daily. It could be because of geography; an initial core belief being stoked (like how to worship) or limited access to varying vantage points for some reason. It could also be that this is the only reality that they have known.

The other side is more immune to the mass programming of society. They most likely have moved out of their small group through travel, education or being ousted for showing up different. They rely more on their first or secondhand information and have outgrown the heavy influences of mass hypnotism and psychic intrusion that the other side is more susceptible to. Their vantage point seems so foreign to the other side.

They also have more compassion for the other side since that is where they originated. At one time, most of society was easily coerced into conformity. Those who are still subdued in conformity resent those who are outgrowing it because that is what they are conditioned to do as a means of preventing more people from defecting. The thought of not having a core means to control factions is terrifying to the factions that control.

When I came back to the world after a year of societal stimuli deprivation, it changed my vantage point. One of the oddest triggers I remembered was with the crucifix. I grew up Catholic and did my rosaries like all good loving people of the "right religion." But when I got re-acclimated to society, I saw the crucifix in an alarming way. It became an open threat against me and all people who speak truth saying, "If you speak against the church, this will happen to you."

There are all these cues we are taught as part of society. My little form of rebellion is when I see a commercial telling people to eat all the bacon they can and challenging their masculinity, I infuse the image with my own and send it into the collective thought stream. I overlay all attempts to overindulge in bacon with images of innocent pigs suffering in small cages.

Just the same way the images were pumped into my television, I send out images of the suffering pigs into the psychic streams to negate the effects of seeing images of sizzling bacon. I send it right back out to everyone who is watching the commercial.

So, everyone who is supposed to be swayed into eating meat by the images is getting the balance of the imagery of suffering pigs as well. That way their conscience can be more easily triggered than if they were just manipulated into primal mode.

This may not prevent mass suffering on its own, but it is something I can do to create a shift in the world without fueling the issue more through judgment and disdain.

SPIRITUAL TRANSFORMATION

*S*piritual *Malpractice*
Detachment as it is presently taught is misleading. Spiritual students are taught to not interfere with the experiences of another so as not to rob them of a life lesson that they need. But this was not taught to help in the spiritual growth of the chela. This was taught in lieu of teaching the student how to really perceive in energy and to discern for themselves.

If one was taught to perceive in energy, they would be able to discern when they are being duped or when assistance is truly warranted. They would even be able to see the interactions that stroke their ego or call them to serve as an agent of the Universe. One hones their own spiritual skills by their interactions with others.

The practice of detachment is a means to prevent a spiritual student from getting over their head or immersed in a negative quagmire that they could not get free of. As a practice, it also prevented the student from inviting a harmful energy into the group dynamics. Or could it possibly have been to trap the most advanced spiritual seekers and the world in an apathetic state?

This practice of detachment has created apathy in the spiritual community that keeps any group trapped in the lower worlds. The apathy that we are seeing in the world is a direct reflection of the apathetic practice of being detached in assisting souls who are suffering. It is devoid of love or compassion.

Maybe the detachment that was taught only worked to a degree if you have transcended the ego. But as long as one is still grappling with the lower worlds, their understanding is going to lead to an apathetic state because that is what an ego does; it quantifies and compartmentalizes. It creates a process devoid of the heart.

Detachment, as it is taught, is an indifference to suffering. It is a cruel, apathetic state of allowing the suffering to continue unhindered or unchallenged. Some of the most spiritual people I know still ascribe to a detachment. What they don't realize is that detachment is being taught wrong.

Just like you would not walk by a puppy that was starving and chained up to a post in the elements, you can have that same discretion with humans that are suffering as well. The fact that the puppy doesn't appreciate the help and tries to bite you doesn't deter you from helping the puppy. It is similar with humans.

Many humans don't have the spiritual tools to free themselves. They have been immersed in programming and conditioning, subjugated to fear tactics, and manipulated by mass hypnotism and psychic influences. They are suffering as much as the puppy in the elements. Do you not help them?

The detachment is foregoing immersing yourself in the stagnant energy that they are trapped in. But it doesn't need to be an all-or-nothing state. Detachment does not mean allowing others to suffer for their own good. It means assisting them from a vantage point where you are not going to be pulled down to their level and trapped yourself. That is what the taps that I post do.

We are in a new evolutionary era now. The apathy that we have created by totally staying removed from others' suffering, we no longer have the luxury to afford. We are all the collective. We must take an interest in the wellbeing of all souls so that we ourselves can thrive. As we awaken and transcend, we make space for others to awaken and transcend. But we do not totally awaken without seeing our reflection in the plight of others.

No longer does spirituality entail just getting out of the body as a form of avoidance and superiority. Spirituality means staying in your body, grounded and aware and expanding your consciousness at the same time. You are aware enough to see that your love, compassion, fortitude, resiliency and integrity are reflected in all other beings and the world itself.

When you refuse to see the suffering in others, you are inducing yourself into an unnecessary slumber. As you use your intentions to better others, you strengthen your own fortitude and conviction and heighten your awakening. As you also better yourself, you better the dynamics of the world and all its inhabitants as well.

THE EPIPHANY

There is the belief that overtaxing the rich is so unfair. I have not challenged it in myself. True, the plethora of poverty, need, illness and inequality in social standing is unfair. But is it fair to put that on the wealthy?

In my mind, it has been an unequivocal no. I have not challenged that belief just like I had never challenged the existence of God or the constructs of family. But maybe everything we silently agree with needs to be overturned and scrutinized.

Just like a person's concept of family and God should be upgraded as they grow and become individualized, so should this concept of feeling like society is victimizing the rich if they are taxed. It would seem that way if the top one percent were merely living a good life and minding their own business. But that is not what is happening.

The top one percent uses their resources to change the narrative of the whole world to bend to their advantage. They use their wealth to demonize the disenfranchised and sway popular opinions in regard to big issues like global warming and reproductive rights. They have been using their advantage of wealth to hold the rest of the world hostage to their political, religious and economical point of view.

It is time for the rich to stop being considered the victim if they are taxed. At this point in our evolvement as a collective community, we must take the unfair advantage away from them that they have used to put us all in danger as a whole, and at a major disadvantage in our sub-sects.

Instead of worrying about what the consequences are to the very rich for being taxed, we must now look at taxation as a survival tool for humanity. We must start giving the same deference to every individual that we have held for the rich. They are no sacred cow. In general, they are a most dangerous group to the freedoms of the individual.

I know this sounds like a great overgeneralization. But this is the same overgeneralization that we all have been divided into in some way or some form. It is time to level the playing field in regard to the rich and hold them accountable for their actions. Taxing their wealth to get a little more of it out of their hands may be what needs to be done.

In so many ways, we have been more compassionate to walking on eggshells in regard to taking the wealth of the rich. But they deserve the same regard as the rest of us in this way. Their fingers must be taken out of the cookie jars of entitlements. They have held us hostage way too long.

If taxing is a way to squelch their incredible ability to drive the narrative of society, we must regain our voices and options as individuals and take back our empowerment.

Decide for Yourself

Another way to look at socialism is individuals taking back their power. It may be beneficial to cap the resources of filthy rich people who use their finances to derail the narrative of the masses. The wealthy at the very top are the ones who are lying about climate control, forcing their morality on reproductive rights and demonizing the sharing of truth.

Perhaps a high tax rate for the top one percent will take away their fodder to highjack the mentality of the masses. Let's fund the arts, creativity, and expressiveness of humanity. Worship of the dollar has to stop. Perhaps the only way to put more value on people is to pour the almighty dollar back in their direction.

If you have a strong reaction to what I am saying here, it's because you have been conditioned by the narrative paid for by the top one percent. Wouldn't it be refreshing to live among people who really could discern for themselves? That is where awakening occurs.

WHY THE SHUTDOWN?

It is a formula move. Those in power, who abuse power, need to create suffering to fuel their position in power. It may not be innately understood by the idiot in charge. It may just be instinct. But he understands to inflict suffering to fuel his position of power. Everything that he does is instinctively done to feed his own position of power.

That was the real reason behind taking the babies away from their mothers at the border. What a great way to create suffering and use a demographic that he devalues. That is the whole purpose of creating such atrocities. That is his purpose for his incitement of the outmoded practice of tribalism. He has been following the playbook of Hitler himself. I would not be surprised if he secretly admired Hitler as he admires the most ruthless dictators of our time.

The suffering of the Jewish people was fodder to keep Hitler in power. This was a horrific time in human history that unfortunately the president idiot in charge is trying to emulate. He is trying to breathe life into past engrams (Akashic recordings of past life issues) to incite fear and suffering to fuel his position of power.

It is time for all individuals to understand the dynamics in energy, so they are not at a disadvantage. At this level of our evolution, many of us are aware enough to address the taking of energy so that we are not put in the same position as we were in past times. For example, many people romanticize Atlantis.

But the subjugating of others and harvesting of their energy was a common practice in Atlantis that created the imbalance that brought their natural demise. It is like the Universe stepped in to stop it. But now we have the awareness to address the practice now. Many of us were in Atlantis and felt helpless. This present life is a redo for many of us who sat by helpless in the times of Atlantis.

Here is how. Do this exercise to support all those who are being targeted for suffering. We are not at the mercy of the head idiot. He is actually doing us all a favor by teaching the masses how irrelevant he is. Sure, he can play his misogynist games to bring hardship to brown people and FBI families (who he blames for his legal troubles and who are affected by the shutdown), but we can do damage control here.

Doing the work here is a means to address issues in energy and to teach you how to take back your empowerment. There are stages for awakening. For some, just seeing through the facade that the head idiot is not legit is a huge catharsis. Another stage is realizing that we do not have to accept the reality that he is trying to inflict on the world. The third stage is to hold him accountable.

(Say each statement three times while tapping on your head and say it a fourth time while tapping on your chest.)

"We convert all fear and trauma into acts of kindness; in all moments."

"We dissipate all suffering with the sanctity of our caring; in all moments."

"We release feeding the abuse of powers with our drama; in all moments."

"We dissipate the force of the energetic blows wielded at the innocent; in all moments."

"We thwart the revival of engrams of suffering and tragedy; in all moments."

"We thwart feeding power factions through tribalism; in all moments."

"We transcend all tribalism; in all moments."

"We withdraw all our agreement from abuses of power; in all moments."

"We send all the effects of ignoble intentions back onto the sender; in all moments."

"We bury the most egregious abusers of power in the backwash of the effects of their own egregious intentions; in all moments."

"We shift our paradigm from helplessness to empowerment; in all moments."

IT'S NOT YOUR PAIN; It's Ours

Many people are suffering and don't realize that it isn't their own. They feel the pain and mental agitation and then try to attribute a reason. Sometimes, maybe most times, maybe all times the issues aren't ours to own. They are part of the collective experience.

If people understood this in general, there would be a lot less pain afflicted on others because people would get the direct correlation between the pain in the world and their own circumstance. Oppression and torture would become obsolete.

Enjoyment of hunting or eating meat would become less desirable because all the suffering that animals do at our hands would be eradicated if it couldn't be compartmentalized away as irrelevant to us. All the awful ways we treat each other could not be filed away and condoned through compliance. People would know the suffering in the world was related to them.

People wonder why children get horrible life-threatening diseases when they are so innocent. Perhaps the innocents are more susceptible to the suffering of the collective. Perhaps their openness and natural kindness allow them to process more suffering out of the collective.

Perhaps the reason that animal meat is considered so carcinogenic is because of the emotional trauma that the animal has endured in being rendered food. There is a lot of pain in caging an animal for life and depriving it of its quality of life. Perhaps the reason so many people are allergic to milk is because they are experiencing the heartbreaking trauma of a newborn being taken away from her mother and the mother being raped of her sustenance intended for her baby. Perhaps this anguishing trauma that people give little regard is imbued in the milk.

The correlation between emotional pain and physical pain is real. When the body systems can't handle any more emotional pain, it manifests as physical symptoms in the body. The emotional issues become like heavy fruit in the body that metastasizes into cysts and growths. If there is a correlation between our own suffering and the collective, then there is also a correlation between our healing and others as well.

Perhaps it is a radical notion to think that anything we do could bring about incredible changes to all of humanity. But it can be no sillier than sitting on the sidelines of life and watching the insanity around us occur without doing anything about it.

(Say each statement three times while tapping on your head and say it a fourth time while tapping on your chest.)

"We extract all suffering from the collective; in all moments."

"We extract all ignorance from the collective; in all moments."

"We extract all tribalism from the collective; in all moments."

"We extract all hatred from the collective; in all moments."

"We extract all misery from the collective; in all moments."

"We extract all depression from the collective; in all moments."

"We extract all addiction from the collective; in all moments.'

"We extract all slavery from the collective; in all moments."

"We extract all programming and conditioning from the collective; in all moments."

"We extract all lack from the collective; in all moments."

"We extract all poverty from the collective; in all moments."

"We extract all disease from the collective; in all moments."

"We extract all war from the collective; in all moments."

"We extract all illusion and limitations around death from the collective; in all moments."

"We extract all manipulation and control from the collective; in all moments."

"We extract all apathy from the collective; in all moments."

"We extract the collective story; in all moments."

"We extract the collective ego; in all moments."

Remember that you are a part of the collective. So, you may feel lighter and empowered in doing these taps. Because just shifting your vantage point from helpless to empowered is a huge form of healing.

DYNAMIC WORK

The energies that attack freedom are subversive. They are taking place on a subliminal level. Those that have more subtle perceptions are able to perceive the onslaught better. Those who still operate in the realms of hope and blind faith are more susceptible to being deceived.

The taps and posts that I share are awakening people on a deeper level than the level of the subversive attacks. The attackers understand the dynamics that happen on the astral realm because power mongers have used them effectively for so long. They have little understanding of the dynamics of energy at a deeper level or of spiritual law. They just know what has worked.

People who understand the work that I do, and the dynamics of it have an edge on those that attack. Pure energy work is much more sophisticated than the manipulations that are occurring on the astral level.

The beauty of the exercises that I share is that they work at a profound level and teach people to perceive in energy while also bypassing the bands of fear that have immobilized the masses into inaction. Those who do the taps that I post are accessing their omnipotence before having conscious understanding of what that entails. The self-realization comes later in most cases and in a more gentle way than without the taps.

The power mongers are at a disadvantage in understanding why their means of control are no longer working. They have been getting more obvious and aggressive with their assaults on humanity as a result. They have little understanding that the psychic energy they are attempting to harness through their cruelty is being dissipated by our work and returned to the individuals in the collective.

The work that I do is incapable of being used in a negative way. It is not something that can be used in turn to enslave humanity. It is because the level of awareness that it works at is a level that is beyond reproach. There is an energetic safe catch involved to prevent that from happening.

The work that I share does not make me richer or more empowered in anyway. I am not taking from the individuals in any way by the sharing. People have become so savvy to being used and would have sensed being used or abused if it were happening. There are no filters on my work or psychic glean put in it to entrap people into giving up an aspect of themselves.

Everything I share is a means of assisting the individual in becoming more individualized and free. It takes energy work of such a pure intention to work more deeply than all the myriad means of control that have been used to enslave the masses thus far. I am not asking for a pat on the back or a thank you.

People just need to know what the next level of service is that is happening to assist humanity in awakening. It is a means to recognizing their own contribution and forgoing the old consciousness of need for validation or praise. If you can see a behavior that the present power mongers display, know that avoiding that behavior and all its distant cousins is a means to quicken your awakening.

In fact, the fact that so many dynamic individuals are living without attracting money is a means of separating them from the vibration of the power that money has been merged with. The natural process of evolving is to purge the vibration of money so that it isn't tainted with power.

The way that this happens is to change the intention of money from taking to giving. The more people use their financial abundance to assist others and to outflow, the more the vibration of money will change from a negative charge to a positive one.

When someone feels they need money or are desperate for money and it doesn't come, the Universe or their innate wisdom is assisting them in not taking on the negative attributes of money inadvertently. It is a form of protection. Instead of wanting money, set out the intention for the goal for which you wanted to use the money.

The desire for money is a block to all your attainable goals. People are not setting their goals with the Universe for what they want. They are setting their goals to have money to get what they want. This is putting a blockage to attaining their goals.

Instead of asking for money to buy your dream home, set out the intention to have your dream home. Remove the dependency on money from the equation. This is trying to micromanage the Universe. This has been the trap that so many have fallen into. The Universe is not a banking system.

The Universe can manifest anything that you desire. But if you desire an upgrade in your vibration, trying to do it through money is working against so many because money has collected such a negative charge. To have money would be a downgrade. If you understand spiritual law at all, using something that has a negative charge to attain a higher vibratory position doesn't work.

To the aware who understand this, they can now see that asking for money is asking for a more negative vibration. Unless you can neutralize your personal relationship with money to neutralize its charge, then it is not an upgrade. But that is not what people do. They ask for money in need and desperation and this is like asking to dumb down their own vibration.

The quickest way to purify the vibration of money is to make it more fluid. Give generous tips and use money to empower others and feel good about your ability to assist. Hoarding money creates stagnation as real and as fruitless as stagnant water.

Dislodge the stagnant pipelines of money that are contaminating energetic channels. Look at the earth from an overview. See the dark channels of money that are clogging up most interactions around the world. See the dark stagnant pools of it in the nexuses of power mongers. Visualize a golden snake that unclogs drains and run it through the channels of humanity.

Unclog all the areas where the dark money has created nests of power. Flush them out. Flush them all out and visualize the golden, clear energy running through all main channels and then all channels. This is profound work. We are changing the vibration of the planet and lessening that control that has been used to enslave us. This is powerful energy work.

It's Beyond Reiki

I facilitated a long-distance healing session with someone from a war-torn country. Since her English wasn't very good, she wanted me to do the healing and instruct her through instant message. She had experienced a low-grade fever for a good part of her life and experienced excruciating fibromyalgia.

As soon as I tuned into her, I felt shards of glass all over her body. I saw explosions strapped to her body in a past and saw that she had blown herself up. I was feeling the shards of glass in her and she was very anxious to get relief. She was a bit impatient.

There is a process to healing. It is not through magic. Some of the dissipation of stagnant energy may be through a form of osmosis. But the very real pain has to register the shift in energy and, with such an entrenched muscle memory of pain, feeling the effects of a release can be a delayed reaction.

I gave the client a whole bunch of taps to do with the Energetic Cleanse. Part of what I do in a private session is to teach the individual to be self- sufficient and not need to depend on healers the rest of their life. This elevates the world in having so many aware individuals as part of the collective.

The client was so impatient that after the session, she got on a healing site and asked for prayers. I was so frustrated about this. The client was getting relief with the work we had done, but the pain came back. The reason the pain came back is because the work we had done was removing the stagnant energy of the issues they were carrying, but when she asked for prayers, all that we were releasing was being backed up by the incoming prayers.

Energy healing is great. But throwing energy at someone is not effective unless the intention is pure, and they are deficient in energy. Many times, when a person has an issue, they have too much stagnant energy in them. They don't need energy added through prayer. They need stagnant energy released through drawing it out. If anyone performs Reiki and has met people who can't sit for the healing, this is why. They need energy released. Not more energy added.

I gave the client a set of taps to do with the Energetic Cleanse (See Chapter 13). I had her do the Energetic Cleanse with all the prayers people had given her. She felt relief in doing this. The pain was gone. She felt lighter. If you have ever asked for prayers, or Reiki, and have felt worse afterwards, perhaps you need the extra energy extracted.

If so, do the Energetic Cleanse with the prayers, Reiki or extra healing energy that you received. Or, if the reaction happened after a certain person worked on you, do the Energetic Cleanse with that person. Perhaps they weren't as clear in that moment as you needed them to be.

THE ANTI-DEMITES

Being compassionate entails the ability to be able to embody the vantage point of another to get an understanding of what it entails. It is not something that some people think about much. It just happens through lifetimes and lifetimes of being at a disadvantage and not wanting to see that pain show up in our lives. Not even in the embodiment of someone else.

The most compassionate people can feel the experience of being destitute, humiliated, forlorn, rejected and demoralized. It is so ingrained in their primal memory banks that they can easily conjure the experience at will when seeing someone else in that circumstance.

They are the ones who are hell bent on helping others. They are literally able to shift vantage points with any other experience and relive it. To be forced to realize that there is so much suffering in the world that is unaddressed is unbearable. Because we are at the stage in our evolution where we not only know of the suffering of others, we can also feel it and embody it as well.

In fact, our expanding understanding of life entails the realization that we are co-mingling with the suffering of others, even if we don't realize it. That strange depression that someone can't shake, the mysterious aches and pains that come out of the blue and the dread and unresponsiveness that happen within relationships are all reflective of what happens in the collective experience. If one wants to eliminate the inconvenience of their own short-lived miseries, they can be less apathetic in the infliction of pain on others.

There are in general two political factions. One is the mentality of 'them versus us' in regard to anyone who is not part of their small tribe. The other one has the understanding that all of life is our tribe. The people who believe in just one life have a very limited vantage point. They put suffering of others and their responsibility to care for others outside of their immediate reference point. The analogy for building a wall is that it is actually keeping out the ability to identify with the plight of others.

I have never understood why Democrats could be demonized. They are the ones who care about others. Why is that such a bad thing? Why is such hate thrown at them? What is wrong with caring about climate change, the quality of life for everyone, or nature, and communities? It is obvious that the hate thrown at caring people must be a projected self-loathing for being so against one's base nature.

Because one's base nature is to care. That is why all the money in the world doesn't satisfy the ravenous hunger of one who is self-serving. Those who are self-serving are serving a primal negative aspect of humanity; one that is desperate to not allow all individuals to awaken because it will die out of its own accord. There is no need to fight those who take as if we are at the same vantage point. They are fighting an inner battle to stay complicit when all of their engrained memories of past atrocities cry out for them to care.

Denial is a hard thing to maintain. All the religious mandates, fear tactics and tainted money can't prevent the human psyche from being swept up in awakening. As the floodwaters of love and compassion flush through the annals of humanity and cleanse the most stubborn bloodstains of want and greed.

So even though one may maintain their vantage point of privilege, the experiences of life will treat them according to their deficiencies. If nothing else, pain and natural discomfort will eventually bring others to the compassion that some already so richly appreciate. If not this lifetime, it will be in another. That is the truth that clings all takers to the one life belief system.

BEING *Proactive Is Being an Activist*

(Say three times while tapping on your head and say a fourth time while tapping on your chest.)

"We do these taps as a surrogate for the collective; in all moments."

"We make space in this world for the passing of HR8; in all moments."

"We remove all blockages to the passing of HR8; in all moments."

"We remove from office all politicians who are on the take; in all moments."

"We dissipate all psychic streams of energy that prevent common sense legislation in regard to gun control; in all moments."

"We thwart the practice of demonizing the victims of gun violence; in all moments."

"We expose all politicians who work as operatives for other countries by taking bribes through the NRA; in all moments."

"We eliminate the false narratives of conspiracy theorists that say that the Sandy Hook massacre never happened; in all moments."

"We thwart the practice of buying and selling America by the pouring of foreign money into the NRA; in all moments."

"We thwart the practice of profiting off of gun proliferation; in all moments."

"We expose all traitors and treason; in all moments."

"We hold all traitors accountable; in all moments."

"We release the normalization of treason; in all moments."

"We strip all credibility off of traitors; in all moments."

"We dissipate the practice of demonizing the just; in all moments."

"We thwart the practice of hiding despicable acts behind religious morality; in all moments."

"We dissipate all psychic streams of energy of religious morality; in all moments."

"We dissipate the practice of hypnotizing the masses using God or religious morality; in all moments."

"We dry up all suffering done directly or indirectly in the name of God; in all moments."

"We release replacing our own inner compass for an outer agenda; in all moments."

"We strip all illusion off of the corrupt and pious; in all moments."

"We release inflicting suffering on immigrants to entrench the mindset and practices of white supremacy; in all moments."

"We awaken all individuals who are hell bent on abusing power, inflicting suffering or entrenched in primal mode; in all moments."

"We hold all individuals in power accountable for their ignoble intentions; in all moments."

"We are centered and empowered in truth, justice, integrity and kindness; in all moments."

FIRE Is Cleansing

It is a fearful time as so many fires burn out of control. All the work I do to save humanity seems not to be working. The mind f@#ks that come through saying that humans aren't worth saving if they don't stop their selfish ways are incredible.

Only half of it is the selfish people who are destroying the planet for profit. They don't care. They have invented a machine to take carbon out of the air. They are okay with artificial air, artificial food, and artificial life.

The rest of the problem is you. You, not realizing your God aspect and with it, your God abilities. You sit on the sideline helpless and now concerned. All the while I have been trying to train people through my taps and visualizations how to access their empowerment.

But I am not entertaining enough, the message is too harsh, I am offensive in some way. So, you read things that make you feel good about life in general. Usually, they are written by a man with a winning persona. But most messages want to placate you or create a follower of you

What I do is teach you to be empowered. Bypass the ego so you can see the magnificent effects of shifting outer circumstances. Sure, you will do the taps to attract money or help your family, but you get put off when I am so intense.

Well now you are getting a glimpse of why I am so intense. I have been living with the reality that some of you are just waking up to; that unless more people wake up and stop pretending they are powerless, we are not going to survive as a planet.

If you sit back and do nothing, then you are deadweight for all the young people and avatars that incarnated now to awaken humanity so this world can continue to exist. If you don't know how to be empowered, do a set of taps I post to try things out. Go to my website and download the free Energetic Cleanse and do the exercise for all the negative things in the world that you are concerned about.

When I try to share the Energetic Cleanse with light workers, I get blocked from pages for self-promoting. Their first reaction is to demonize me for posting it. The time when people are responsive to me is when I help them get their lost pet home. Do these animal lovers realize how many millions of furry families are being destroyed in the fires?

There is a positive spin on current affairs. Maybe the fires are burning off layers and layers of hate and greed that have accumulated on the planet. Maybe it is burning them off for good. Maybe people are waking up to their own role in allowing themselves to be complacent in what happens in the world. Why should anyone have less of a voice than anyone else?

People don't have the luxury of sitting back and saying it's not their problem. They don't have the luxury of saying that it's not my kids dying. We are all feeling the effects of so much turmoil in the world. We no longer have the luxury of feeling displaced, unheard, unwanted or victimized. That is what bullies want us to feel when we show such inner strength.

And you, in your empowerment, are a threat to all the scumbags in the world who prop themselves up with money and hide behind religion or some other entitlement bravado as rationale for their selfishness. You can decide to awaken or not. You can activate your God energy just by visualizing good outcomes.

Do taps to oust the power mongers. Imagine a billion trees being planted. See the oceans being purified. Hold space in your thoughts and imagination for nature to return. Plant a tree in your neighborhood. Instead of praying for things or asking for prayers, use your intentions to see the whole world green and thriving.

When I hear someone asking for prayers these days, I get annoyed. It just shows up as an attention-getter for someone who feels validated by having something worth asking for prayers for. One person can do the healing on another. It doesn't take mass sympathy to get it done. That actually works against healing. To announce a personal issue of someone else and have strangers put their interpretations on what a loved one is experiencing is a violation of spiritual law.

I almost died this week. I know telling you seems like a contradiction, but it would help you to know what is being done by individuals to assist humanity in awakening. I did not want anyone to know who would have entrenched their opinions on me. The energy work I do is to dissipate the psychic energy that has been allowing the power mongers to lead us into nuclear war.

What you see playing out now, I saw years ago. That is why I seem so intense and am so harsh to those who backslide. It is frustrating to have people retain the information I give them but then get worked over by their own ego and then compartmentalize the work with a resentment of me. I don't have the social skills to placate the fragile human consciousness. If it is between that and addressing the psychic energies that disregard quality of life, I am going to stay focused on what I am doing energetically.

I understand that this all sounds harsh, but if the forests of the world don't pierce the layers of apathy preventing you from activating your God Force, then maybe some stark words will do the trick.

'I love you,' is not a warm and fuzzy sentiment. It is a Mission Statement at this point. I love you enough to put myself out there and throw everything I am at the wall to try to assist you in awakening to your own God potential. I have seventeen books out there to help you; I post techniques every day. I share as much truth as I can.

I also have a retreat coming up. I know inwardly a lot of you have been called to attend. But outwardly you refuse to show up. It's fear of getting pulled into something, money issues or excuses like other commitments.

It is so frustrating for me to offer these things on behalf of the Ancient Ones, seeing all the lifetimes of people starving for truth and knowing that what I share is the real reason people have incarnated this lifetime, only to have people have a conflict in coming because of a commitment to a picnic or some other reason.

So many lifetimes you have cried out for truth, love and a connectedness. The retreats are a means to access all of those things within yourself. It is also a huge boost of higher vibration for the planet. I would love the synergy of your presence.

I love you.

BEYOND ALL ILLUSION

❧

*A*ddressing *Gang Violence*
     I have wondered why the governments don't deal with the gang violence that is gripping the southern continents and causing so much misery in creating so many refugees. It is ridiculous that so many people are running from their homes and nothing is done to address the issue.

I got my answer watching the current season of Top Chef, believe it or not. All the contestants were introducing themselves. One woman proudly announced that her mother was the shaman of the largest controlling gang in South America.

That was the reason. All these people and governments were held in fear by the gang's energies, not only by their threats and tactics. They were actually using psychic energy to inflict fear and gain control. Someone who perceives in energy has an edge on those who don't.

That is the problem with not educating people on how to protect themselves from psychic energies. It is not government's fault; they do not understand in energy either. What I do here is equip the masses in how to deal with psychic tactics. Anything that can create fear in someone can pull them out of their center and cause them to become susceptible to the tactics of the unethical and the ruthless.

There is nothing to be proud of in enabling gangs. Perhaps we here have enough distance to address the issue easily and efficiently. Dissipating psychic energy is a part of what I do. There really is no secret. You just make your love greater than any fear and the love will evaporate the fear.

When you evaporate the fear, you also strip off the illusion that creates a larger than life facade on any one or issue. Part of what I do here is strip the energy off power mongers that causes them to look larger than life.

Why do you think that all the politicians and those in authority are showing up as criminals and idiots? Why is there no one to admire? The energy that they have accrued by taking it from others has been stripped off of them and given back to the individuals.

That is the fuel individuals have needed to awaken. They were stripped down. Now they are becoming whole for the first time in lifetimes. As incredible as that seems, that is what I am doing here. That is what I am teaching this generation to do by teaching them the SFT taps and the protocol to do it. I have given them a means to take back the energy that has been siphoned off of them by power factions and others who have literally raped their soul. Everyone who does my SFT taps is regaining their strength and empowerment that may have been missing for years.

The tapping exercises I share are allowing individuals to access their inner empowerment beyond the confines of the ego or their petty conditioning. It allows them to be the God Being that they are capable of being before they are able to acknowledge or accept their own empowerment. The more they do the taps and exercises I share, the more they will be able to perceive the more subtle dynamics that their outer five senses dis-allow.

To address the immigrant issue, the gang issue has to be addressed. What these taps that I post are able to do is strip off all the psychic energy that gives gangs and their members a larger than life persona.

It can release the grip of fear that is holding a whole continent hostage.

The energy work that I do is stronger than any shaman or psychic taker. I am positive of that and I have no qualms addressing the negative energies that hold the world hostage in hate. I am a badass in energy and my love is bigger than any fear that they can induce.

As you do this exercise, notice the fear-based thoughts that run through your head. Having these scary thoughts is evidence that the energy work you are doing is effective. The low energies of control have no other option than to induce you to fear. They actually use your own ego against you in this way. That is a huge reason to address the ego and not let it control you.

(Say each statement three times while tapping on your head and say it a fourth time while tapping on your chest.)

"We dissipate the psychic streams of energy that hold gangs in power; in all moments."

"We sever all strings and cords of control that gangs have implemented; in all moments."

"We remove all curses that gang members have implemented; in all moments."

"We strip all illusion off of gangs and all its members; in all moments."

"We disarm all the energy workers of ignoble intentions that have enabled the gangs and their violence; in all moments."

"We strip all gang members and their power sources of entitlement; in all moments."

"We free all gang members from the hell of their indoctrination into the gang; in all moments."

"We dissipate the psychic energy of hate, revenge and justification that fuels the gangs; in all moments."

"We dismantle the psychic power sources that fuel the gangs; in all moments."

"We dismantle all gangs; in all moments."

"We hold all gang members accountable; in all moments."

"We convert all the fear of gangs to love and empowerment; in all moments."

"We free all entrenched souls from the cycle of gang violence; in all moments."

"We dry up all gang violence; in all moments."

"We slap the wrists of all those with ignoble intentions; in all moments."

"We reprimand all those entrenched in ignoble intentions by back-washing their intentions back onto themselves; in all moments."

"We awaken all gang members to their responsibility to humanity; in all moments."

"We empower all gang members to make immediate restitution for all their crimes against humanity; in all moments."

In Thought, *Form or Deed*

I couldn't post on my own group page because they said that some of the information on my page was reported as abusive. This is where we have come.

There are machines out there called bots that are being used as weapons to turn the human mind into a mush of compliance. People don't even realize they are being manipulated. These machines are inundating the psyche and are very savvy in either lulling us into complacency or swaying us to turn against our humanity and attacking those who have a relatively very slight different point of view than we do.

Everything that I post is coming from a living awakened point of view. It is intended to cut through the layers of gummy conditioning and to stir a reaction into your psyche. That is what truth does. People aren't used to truth, so they have a reaction to it. We are supposed to think differently than others. We are supposed to discern truth from our own unique vantage point. That is what I do, and that is what I encourage others to do with my writing.

What they have been conditioned to do is scan all that they take in to find what they already agree with. They have been taught to endorse what they already accept as truth and attack everything that they do not agree with. They have been conditioned to attack. I too get annoyed with propaganda machines that are the job of some media outlets. But that is not what my writing does.

Nor am I angry or abusive in my writing. If something I write causes a reaction in you, you may want to question why. If you agree with a huge part of my writing but something causes a reaction in you, maybe sit back and ask yourself why?

Someone rebuked my writing recently because I used the word scumbag in a tap describing the present president. I explained to him that the harsh word had a certain vibration that matched the energy of what the tap was addressing. There is psychic energy that becomes very thick to wade through emotionally. The taps I post dissipate this energy so that the ether is freer to think in and exercise discernment in.

Since the beginning of this man's election, I have seen things about him and his character that are now being revealed in the news cycles. Things that I know in energy some realize, but they don't add them up and remember them like I do. I remember everything that I learn, and it is accrued in what I tap into as conscious awareness.

What I know is that this person refused to help the people in Puerto Rico and many suffered and died because of his neglect. He has caused and advocated for much suffering at the borders and has committed crimes against humanity in his treatment of families at the border. I feel the suffering that he causes.

His indifference to the suffering perpetuates much more suffering. He uses the position he holds to gain a foothold of power and wealth in the world. His intention (yes, intention in energy as well) was to set himself and his children up as oligarchs in this country. He is still trying to overthrow our longstanding democracy for his own gain.

That was the meaning of his last thumbs up communication to his puppet master. Perhaps the work I do and the taps you have done with me are the things that have prevented this from happening as easily as he thought it would. Those who have done the taps I post may be the reason for his lack of success. Perhaps it is what has caused the ire of others, the undoing of a course that was already set as reality.

He has worked diligently to ruin the reputation of career professionals to suit his own defenses. He is abusive to all who don't agree with him. He intended to set himself up as a modern-day Hitler by refurbishing the engrams (memories of the past) and also creating a modern-day holocaust with the immigrants as the victims.

Those who crave power and wealth and have little concern with the suffering that they cause are technically scumbags. No one will say this out loud because the psychic energy of saying this causes them to either fear the repercussions of saying it, or they have been duped into believing that he is righteous for what he is doing. This is a lie that I see even spiritually advanced people fall into. But I stand by my statement. This individual is a scumbag,

It is true that he is being used as a conduit to awaken the masses out of their complacency. This is a good by-product of what he is doing. But that doesn't make him good. It certainly doesn't mean that what he does needs to be endorsed by those who understand this one truth about him. Or that he was supposed to succeed. Of course, he is breaking up archaic power structures that we all have bought into. That doesn't mean we are supposed to support the power structure he is attempting to put into place.

The whole point of his being used to disrupt the programming we have been conditioned to accept is for us to learn to discern for ourselves. That is the whole point. It is not to be complacent in allowing him to create a structure that causes suffering to others. Those who abuse power and cause suffering innately know that the suffering they cause generates fuel to entrench themselves further in the psyche of humanity. He cannot be allowed to do this. The suffering he has caused has been minimized and he has been prevented from benefiting from it. This is part of the more subtle work I do.

Even the densest person at perceiving in energy knows in their gut that this man is not a good man. They realize the things that he does are harmful to individuals. What they are doing by agreeing to comply with him as a leader is weakening their own innate sense of truth and warping their own inner guidance system. These aware beings bring this to the collective and act as weakening the advancement of spirituality and not strengthening it, as they believe.

They will do this in thinking they are following some spiritual mandate, which is actually a lie that has been purported by some savvy bots that understand the individual's craving for truth. This is not truth but capturing those who crave truth with a more complicated lie. I am amazed at the people who fall for it. Those who crave truth but want it to look a certain way, fall prey to the lateral move of false conspiracy theories.

You may not like what I write. It may offend the conditioning that you grew up with. It may cause you to attack me. I am used to it. I have literally been bred and trained not to feel the regular barbs of attacks that others may experience. My resistance is strong. During my own gestation period, my mother tried to abort me by poisoning me with alcohol. So, whatever is said and done to attack me, things that would devastate others, I will hardly notice. I may even register it as natural.

I just tell you this to help you understand how strong someone needs to be to love people more than they love their own defilement. The defilement in this case is the systemic conditioning to conform. What is written to you here is meant to break up that conditioning.

It is the same conditioning that tells you that you need to perform to be accepted; that you need to have more, be more attractive, smarter, taller or younger to be worthy. That is also a lie. You are loved and valued just as you are. The more unique and different from all the rest in thought, form and deed, the better.

In Response to a Letter from a Young Teen

Thank you so much for writing to me.

I know this sounds like a very scary dream. But it is nothing that I don't deal with regularly. It is part of what I do. It is not scary to me and once I explain, it will seem less scary to you. In fact, exciting. It is true that the government is a faction of power and would prefer to stop me from what I do. They have tried so many times in my life and they have been unable to. It is not people though. It is just a dead energy of habit that is like a memory. It is like a song playing over and over because there is a glitch. They have a limited bag of tricks and I have so many Ancient Beings helping me help others. Helping people is too important and can't be stopped anymore. I have been sent here to do what I do. That is why I have no family or the things that other people value. Because I have nothing to lose in doing the work. The work is in freeing people who are afraid to be empowered.

I get scary scenarios playing through my head sometimes. It is a gauge to me now how much I am making an impact. If I were not making an impact, there would be no need to try to make me afraid. You are learning a very adult lesson. Fear is the only tactic for control. Nobody can ever force you to do what you don't want to do. They can only instill fear and make you do things to yourself. When you are feeling afraid of anything, realize that you are breaking through some kind of limitation. It is your own ego being used to keep you from growing through fear. This is in general and not to be sensed in regards to your parents. You do what they tell you to because of love and respect. Not control. It's a difference. But fear is only a kind of dial for you to gauge how important your spiritual work is. Truth, love and kindness are all spiritual work.

Being afraid is a means to prevent you from being a dynamo. All you have to do is expand how much love you contain. If you are feeling afraid, love more. It does not have to be a sappy sentiment but more with the respect of one martial artist to his teacher. Watch as I just pour my love into you. Feel that confidence and safety? I love you and watch your back constantly. I am able to do that. I have been practicing lifetimes how to make my love so big. You can love me back if you feel comfortable. Your love will help me. It will help me to stretch my love and help more people, animals, trees and the earth itself. It is not like money where it is used to make myself seem more important. That is not possible at this level of healing I don't think.

Now if you feel anything that makes you feel afraid, it is merely stagnant energy that thinks it's a person. It is like a piece of ash that curls as it breaks away and burns a little before it dissipates. Here is a technique to use:

Whatever you are feeling afraid of, name it and then put it into two sentences. As an example, let's use the statement "influence through the computer."

Plug it into these two sentences:

"I send all energy matrices into the Light and Sound that _____; in all moments."

"I command all complex energy matrices that _____ to be escorted into the Light and Sound by my Guides; in all moments."

You would plug in the statement about being influenced through the computer and do the two statements as SFT taps. Meaning you say each statement three times while tapping on your head and say a fourth time while tapping on your chest.

Do the following taps exactly like this:

"I send all energy matrices into the Light and Sound that influence me through the computer; in all moments."

"I command all complex energy matrices that influence me through the computer to be escorted into the Light and Sound by my Guides; in all moments."

There is no need to be afraid of anything. It is people's misunderstanding of what these things are that causes them so much fear. When you realize how easy it is to shift into love instead of fear, it will be as silly to react to such things as it would to be afraid of dust. I promise you. And, of course, I am able to assist you wherever you are and in all moments. Use this technique with anything that makes you afraid. You can even plug in the statement "that causes me to be afraid."

Thank you for your priceless information. I am going to post this answer. Just this answer on my page for others to benefit from what you gain here. Thank you very much for taking the time to write. I love you very much. You are very special to me.

Love,

Jen

BEYOND THE ILLUSION of Earth

There is a reality that exists outside of the illusion of earth. I don't talk about it much because it's best to allow innocence to prevail. Even if it is overwhelming to see the corruption happening on the planet, it is best to allow people to be blissfully unaware of the happenings outside of the illusion of earth.

It is no different than people from a small town not being able to comprehend the workings of a major city that is a hub of international affairs. Some people do tap into the existence outside the realms of the illusion of earth. But they are deemed crazy.

There are also those who desperately seek the truth outside of the illusion of earth. Unfortunately, the seekers are given their information by power factions trying to control earth and enslave all of humanity. They feed those who seek out the conspiracy theories.

Power factions feed them enough truth to bait them and then they add their spin on the truth: the lies that allow them to corrupt and pillage. They tell them things that the seeker would have no way to discredit. They feed on human's fear and outrage to spread the lies. They had almost succeeded.

See? Sounds Crazy. That is why I don't mention it much until it becomes necessary. It is necessary. So many people are being worked on psychically to think that things are hopeless, to feel desperate and even suicidal. This is not a coincidence. No one is alone in feeling hopeless. There is a war that is happening outside of the illusion of earth.

We are fighting to free the literal soul of humanity. That is what I do here. I help people free themselves without their needing to be stripped of their illusion of this world. But the darkness of the galactic war seeps in through the density of the feeling (or vibration) of dark money, religious and political corruption and trafficking.

When I was at the mercy of a psychopath for a year, I was able to tap into all the research he did with different races of humanoids outside of the illusion of earth. It has been very important to under-stand the dynamics of what is happening in the world. Because of my sensitivities and purpose in making others aware, I have had many experiences with the other humanoid species.

The energy work I do frees humans from the psychic grip of these other species. The fact that so many people are awake to the systemic corruption in the world is evidence of a change. The layers of apathy and complacency that we have been wrapped in are being stripped away. More and more people are doing the taps that I post, and this is creating a pocket of clarity in perceptions.

But recently, more and more people are reaching out in despera-tion. They feel hopeless, joyless and depressed. Many people are being bombarded with instructions to kill themselves. They get visuals and encouragement to do it. The thoughts come into their psyche like seeds of thoughts that are being consciously planted by humanoid races that want anyone who is awakening and has the ability to discern truth, to kill themselves.

If you have self-defeating feelings, it is evidence that you are awak-ening. If the energy of hating and attacking others has worn off, it means that you are entering the next level of psychic manipulation. If you really have no inclination to judge or attack others and the fear has burned off, you may have entered the realm of the energies trying to have you kill yourself.

Instead of indulging in those matters, maybe do the taps to strip the psychic control that the other species have inflicted on humanity. We have been groomed many lifetimes to be lulled into a false sense of complacency. The other races have been pumping lies into our culture since our beginning. That is why when we pray, we send our energy out to these other humanoid species.

From my personal experience with these humanoid species, I can tell you the names I have given them for reference. One of them that show up as sultry women are androgynous. I call them cat people, but they have nothing to do with earth cats. They have a feeling to them like the cat women on the old Batman show. But they are so devious that they may be the root reason why women have been demonized and why transgender people are so feared.

There are four different humanoid races that have been affecting those who are still ignorant of the corruption in our government. They have been working in synergy to maintain control of ever-awakening humans. The four factions have been propping up the power factions on this hemisphere. But there are others that have been propping up the other ruthless dictators of the world.

If you want to really assist the awakening of humanity, these foreign factions must be addressed. These taps that I share strip away the illusion that these races have engulfed each individual in. Those that seem so far from truth are being affected by these factions. So are our top leaders.

If you want to make a difference in the awakening of humanity do as many of these sets of taps as possible. See the Energetic Cleanse in Chapter 13 and insert one of these phrases in all the sentences and do all the taps. Some will be harder to do. These are the ones that are most important to do.

- The cat people
- The bird people
- The spider people
- The lizard people
- The synergy between the cat, bird, spider and lizard people
- The synergy of the humanoid species propping up the corrupt
- The cyborg races
- The synergy between the three cyborg races
- The cyborg races working through the corrupt

If you have been depressed, feeling hopeless, having thoughts of suicide, gather your strength to do these taps. See how it helps lighten your outlook. You can refer others to the cleanse at https://www.jen-uinehealing.com/energetic-cleanse-sign-up-f.../

. . .

Don't Allow the Whales to Die

Imagine you were enjoying the peace and quiet of your home and suddenly an air raid sound went off. But it just didn't go off for a while. It was a continuous presence in your home, and you had to get used to it, suffer or die. This is the fate waiting for the whale population in the Atlantic because the current president has approved seismic testing. The greed mongers want to look for oil under the surface of the ocean and are planning to bombard water life with sound to find it.

This will kill off many species. They won't be able to handle this intrusion. This is where the rubber meets the road, people. This is where people can choose to wallow in the selfishness and greed of this society by their indifference, or they can take back their voice and stand up to the power mongers who are desecrating our existence. You choose the quality of life for yourself and generations to come.

This is the incarnation that is important. What we allow to transpire will affect the world for generations to come. What we prevent from transpiring will allow the quality of life on earth to continue to be organic. Please use your voice by doing these taps.

(Say each statement a total of four times. The first three times tap the top of your head, and the fourth time tap the middle of your chest.)

"I declare myself a surrogate for the world inhabitants in doing these taps; in all moments."

"We gift the power mongers with the sensitivities of an empath; in all moments."

"We strip all denial off of the world in dealing with power mongers; in all moments."

"We dissipate the systemic indifference that allows power mongers to desecrate the earth; in all moments."

"We release allowing power mongers to destroy the earth; in all moments."

"We send all energy matrices into the light and sound that enable seismic testing; in all moments."

"We command all complex energy matrices that enable seismic

testing to be escorted into the light and sound; in all moments."

"We sever all strings and cords between ourselves and seismic testing; in all moments."

"We recant all vows and agreements between ourselves and seismic testing; in all moments."

"We remove all curses between ourselves and seismic testing; in all moments."

"We remove all blessings between ourselves and seismic testing; in all moments."

"We sever all strings, cords and wires between ourselves and seismic testing; in all moments."

"We dissolve all karmic ties between ourselves and seismic testing; in all moments."

"We remove all vivaxes between ourselves and seismic testing; in all moments."

"We strip power mongers of all their ignoble intentions; in all moments."

"We crumble all constructs mandated by power mongers; in all moments."

"We nullify all contracts with seismic testing; in all moments."

"We strip all illusion off of seismic testing; in all moments."

"We eliminate the first cause in seismic testing; in all moments."

"We close all portals for seismic testing; in all moments."

"We release being locked in agreement with seismic testing; in all moments."

"We relinquish the ruthless pursuit of seismic testing; in all moments."

"We release resonating or emanating with seismic testing; in all moments."

"We extract all of seismic testing from our Sound Frequency; in all moments."

"We extract all of seismic testing from our Light Emanation; in all moments."

"We extract all of seismic testing from all 32 layers of our energy field; in all moments."

"We extract all of seismic testing from our whole beingness; in all moments."

"We shift our paradigm from seismic testing to organic earth living; in all moments."

"We transcend seismic testing; in all moments."

"We are centered and empowered in organic earth living; in all moments."

"We infuse organic earth living into our Sound Frequency; in all moments."

"We imbue organic earth living into our Light Emanation; in all moments."

"We resonate, emanate and are interconnected to all life in organic earth living; in all moments."

Please share these with others and ask them to personally do them. Please know you are empowering goodness and kindness in doing these. It is necessary now.

PREVENT *the Mother of All Holy Wars*

The process of awakening is to drop out of the trappings of conditioning that keep us distracted from our spirituality. Everything that we know and believe was conditioned into us. At first, it was for survival, but then it became a form of control.

One of the easiest ways to control any group is to split it into two opposing factions and pit them against each other. This happens in families when a parent will pit the children against each other to keep them loyal to the parent.

We see this happening in politics right now. No matter what our vantage point is, we find ourselves being demonized as the enemy. We may also find ourselves swept up in demonizing others with opposing views.

Since the global reach of our awareness is so expansive, we are no longer fighting with the tribe that borders us. We are being divvied up into bigger and bigger factions. It is imperative for the power factions to control the narrative and keep us pitted against each other.

There is a desperate attempt to keep us entrenched in infighting even if the infighting has a global reach. It is a means to prevent the mass awakening to which we are all looming.

If any of this speaks to you as truth, please do the following list of taps to prevent the world from being entrenched in a global holy war. I am able to read the Akashic Records of the planet. Doing these taps directly shifts the course of the planet and nudges it towards world peace.

1) Refer to the Energetic Cleanse in Chapter 13.

2) Start each set of taps with the following statement:

"I declare myself a surrogate for humanity in doing these taps."

Say it three times while tapping on your head and say it a fourth time while tapping on your chest.

3) Do the Energetic Cleanse with the following list. (Please resist the urge to take sides and only do half the taps. Do the whole list.)

- Christian warfare
- Muslim warfare
- Harnessing the anguish of indigenous people
- Alt right
- Alt left
- Genocide
- All Holy Wars
- Psychic warfare
- Cyber warfare
- Nuclear war
- Desecrating the land
- Raping the land
- Gutting humanity
- The Dark ages
- Primal mode
- Enslaving the masses

What Other Planets *Think of Us*

We are considered a planet of barbarians compared to other planets' standards. In fact, we are a great intergalactic experiment. There are some very compassionate species that support our survival. There are other species that think we are not worth the trouble and we should be left to destroy ourselves.

The species that support our continued existence have lent a strand of their DNA to help us awaken to our potential. There are dark factions that have wished to control us. They have worked throughout governing and religious systems to keep us enslaved to a very limited perception of ourselves.

Worshiping up to the sky was something we were taught by factions that wanted us to fail in realizing our own potential. This one exercise keeps us diluting our energy by sending it out to some unknown source.

One of the tools for continued survival is the ability to change vantage points. It affords one the ability to grasp any point of view. Without knowing it, one is exercising omniscience in doing this. That is what compassion does. It allows us to experience what someone is experiencing from their vantage point while maintaining our stance in our own.

Those species who are threatened by our existence want to see us fail. They want to see us destroy ourselves. They realize that the way to prevent our awakening is to stay entrenched in one specific viewpoint that negates others. There are factions working so hard to keep us steeped in ignorance.

When one is close-minded, can't fathom another's point of view, judges and demonizes others, they show little growth on the evolutionary scale. Love expands consciousness. Fear contracts it. Pay attention to all the signals and reminders that program us to be fearful. Some of them are hidden behind self-righteousness.

Our whole political and religious system is based on fear. There is fear of the enemy, fear of the unknown, fear of death, fear of our own actions and fear to question. We have been conditioned to remain in primal fear. More of us are needed to choose love and awakening over fear. This is the means to our continued survival. It is a choice.

People may say that they love this country. But unless they love the inhabitants of the country and the planet itself, they are showing their programming and hypocrisy. It is not Love to divide people, ignore their needs, split them into factions and demand blind loyalty.

Those of us who are able to love, must love with such an expansive quality that it dissipates the psychic energy of rhetoric that hold so many in bondage to ignorance. To survive, we must love enough to dissipate the fear. It is not a luxury or a quaint musing. Love is the most dynamic force in the Universe. It must be enacted for our survival.

THE PSYCHIC PLOY

I have all these interesting dreams of factions trying to pull the masses back into the herd mentality. When they happen, I am obligated to report back to others the psychic ploys used to try to prevent them from finding truth.

In one dream, I was walking the route of a truth seeker. I was going to all the places that people go when they are searching for truth. I was meeting very interesting young people. There was one young woman who seemed like she would be a best friend. She was very friendly to me and she seemed to care about nature. But when we were walking, she didn't seem bothered that they were cutting down a lot of trees to put up houses. This struck me as odd.

There was a young Asian American man that I met who was very personable and likeable. He seemed to understand what all young people know. He was likable but intimidating with his ease. After I met him, I ended up visiting a small shop in an eclectic part of town. I was interested in buying certain essential oils to remedy hair loss.

Hair loss is symbolic because it is one of those things that as much as people want to salvage their hair, they believe that going bald is inevitable. Hair loss symbolized spiritual truth. In the dream, I knew of the cure for hair loss. I went to the shop to get the ingredients and I was willing to share what I knew on how to regrow hair (attain spiritual truth).

I showed the pattern of baldness. I explained how the oils revitalize the hair shafts. I was very free in educating the man behind the counter of what I knew. He didn't engage me at all with anything about hair loss (truth). In fact, he seemed disinterested. His goal was just to attend the shop as little as possible.

This shop owner was an attractive Asian American. He looked like an Asian Ray Liotta. I asked him what his cure was for hair loss. But he was evasive. He was engaging but never did give me the formula he used. I sensed he really didn't have one. Instead, he sent me to a meeting that would give me all my answers. In the dream, he showed up Asian because there is a belief that other cultures know more of truth than we do. The dream was blatantly debunking this fallacy.

Before leaving, I asked him about his culture and if he respected his grandmother. She represented the wisdom of Gaia. He said he gave deference to her in theory, but it was more an antiquated respect. He said that he didn't listen to her at all and did his own thing. It was telling me that male energy may show up seemingly balanced and pretending to have an understanding of Gaia, but it is only an outer pretense and not true respect for a great source of truth.

I showed up at the meeting that he sent me to where I could learn all the secrets of what he sold. It was held in the building that used to be the center for a spiritual group that I had outgrown already. (What they were teaching was old information.) The meeting was run by his younger brother. It was showing the nepotism still involved in seeking truth. Being run by his younger brother showed how truth is still being packaged by male energy to keep one engaged in the group mentality.

The woman I made friends with was in the meeting, but she was very standoffish and wouldn't talk to me. She had a petty grudge against me somehow. It was showing how women are still operating in male energy. They were not embracing their Goddess energy at all. She wasn't anyways. It was showing how the group mentality does not honor Gaia.

There was a light show on the wall. The young man operated a projector and threw this colorful image onto the wall. It was considered high tech. The meaning of this is just because a group talks about the Light and Sound of God, doesn't mean they know how to assist the seeker in engaging with it.

Just talking about the Light and Sound of God doesn't make one cutting edge. The facilitator and his group had no understanding of how to engage spiritually so they reduced it to a passive presentation. That is what we see in groups that speak about the Light and Sound of God but don't teach the individual how to operate beyond the ego as a Light emanation or a Sound frequency. Issues like taking on karma are obsolete when you embrace you own nature, which is beyond form.

There was also a member of my old spiritual group at the meeting, just in case I didn't understand the message. If someone shows up in a dream that you know but not intimately, the dream is conveying to you a message using your assessment of that person. This person was very kind and likeable, but he thought he was superior to others. His goal in the group was to be respected like a grand poobah.

He was showing the intention of the group was still to create a pecking order with the individuals subjugated in some subtle form. The group members can be told that they are being empowered and they can believe it. But as long as they are being taught to give allegiance to anyone outside of themselves, they are still being subjugated.

The whole dream was conveying something very important about spiritual groups. Spiritual groups do not change. There is a movement here to add new ideals to old groups to refurbish them. This does not work. The old tenets of any group are the underlining factors of what that group is about.

Most groups were forged in the steel of male dominance. They may try to convince you that they have evolved. But they are just using new ideals of female empowerment to reengage you in their male dominated sect. Female empowerment does not need a group to give her merit.

Gaia loves all of her children and sends them out in all directions to gain their empowerment. She does not whisper fear in their ears and threaten them if they leave. She does not demand that they worship at her feet and shamelessly stroke a frail ego. She wishes all her sisters and brothers to be empowered to share all that they are without needing to prove themselves again and again through sacrifice or tithe themselves to death.

Gaia knows that all who are empowered in female energy give all that they can of themselves. That is the nature of Gaia. There is no need to mandate worship, service, or tithing because the life of Gaia is a continuous gift. In fact, those who embrace Gaia need to be reminded of self-care because they easily and effortlessly give all that they are to advance the empowerment and betterment of others.

The dream was showing me just another way male energy was whitewashing their controlling ways to maintain control of the masses. If they had to pretend to be compassionate, incorporate alternative practices, throw around popular phrases like Namaste or Enlightenment, and claim to understand the Light and Sound of God, they will, to maintain control.

Any group that pays homage to a male at the core or anyone outside of the individual, is not an enlightened means of finding truth. It is merely another window display for power and control. If there were any faction that was leading people to truth, you would see more evidence of truth and love in the world. We have all been duped now for too long. This dream is showing how that is done.

Empowerment is an individual thing. The tools I share do not lead to worship of a personality. There is no group to engage. There is protection in doing the exercises I post because I give protection unconditionally. It is not something that someone has to pay for or proclaim allegiance for. I assist because I can. Anyone who has my abilities and passion would do the same.

Everyone has to get up from their knees and support the weight of their own empowerment. The truth is waiting for you. There is no need for an interpreter or middleman. Stand on your own spiritual feet and know you are safe and supported in your intentions. Otherwise, why would I bother?

REPAIR YOUR ENERGY FIELD, *Repair the Earth*

(Say three times while tapping on your head and say it a fourth time while tapping on your chest.)

"I remove all interference in the functioning of all my aura mechanics; in all moments."

"I release all dysfunction in all of my aura mechanics; in all moments."

"I remove all schisms between the functioning of all my soul mechanics; in all moments."

"I remove all interference in the functioning of all of the earth's aura mechanics; in all moments."

"I release all dysfunction in all of the earth's aura mechanics; in all moments."

"I remove all schisms between the functioning of all the earth's soul mechanics; in all moments."

THE BLACK MAGICIAN

I have been accused of doing black magic by someone who has little understanding of spiritual law. Let me be clear: the taps I post in no way violate spiritual law or the sanctity of any soul. What they do is combat the black magician who has society duped into submission.

Lack of understanding of the workings of energy is the reason that the black magicians of the world can rape humanity as they do. The long-term remedy is an understanding of the dynamics of energy. The short-term remedy is the taps that I provide to strip away from the black magicians all the energy they have accumulated through ill will.

What I do is in adherence to spiritual law. When you do the taps, you are working as the long hand of the angels and spirit guides that diligently work to prevent us from destroying ourselves and being a nuisance to other worlds.

Do you know what black magic is?

Mass hypnotism

Demonizing the downtrodden

Rhetoric used to divide and bring conflict

Using the collective energy for personal gain

Pitting sects of people against each other to dilute their effectiveness

Using lies as a distraction from the suffering created

Creating suffering to harness the suffering for fuel

Desecrating the sacred ceremonies for personal gain (4th of July)

Demonizing anyone with integrity or the ability to speak the truth

Squelching the voice of the people

Creating a psychic atmosphere of fear

Using fear to maintain power

Dismantling the protective components of the whole

Demonizing and sullying anyone with integrity and valor

Putting one's self on a pedestal

Accruing unearned accolades

Taking credit for things that one has not done

Breaking down the proper order of things

A DIVINING ROD for Awakening

As subtle as it is, fear of taking on karma is still fear. To raise your vantage point even more, a healer has to do what they do with such a purity of purpose that there is no fear of anything.

The fear of being tainted with evil or being inundated with unnecessary energies means that the vantage point isn't high enough to be effective. In fact then, fear becomes a self-check as to where your vantage point is in doing the work.

That becomes the only purpose of fear: an indicator of where your comfort level is. You well realize that love dissipates all fear. So, if you are experiencing fear, it is a means of checking yourself for any beliefs that may hinder your effectiveness.

The vantage point that you work and live at should be one of such profound sacred gratitude that the love in itself is a protection. Nothing can erode away the self-cleansing nature of Sacred Love.

Be in love with all life. Find more ways to express love. Love and kindness must be such an integral part of your make-up that you ascribe the action of loving to your parasympathetic nervous system. This means that loving becomes as natural as breathing.

This is the way to raise the bar on humanity. The more people who emanate love as naturally as breath, the more we will raise the bar on the collective. Others will get it through osmosis. This is how we all bring an abrupt end to the things that cause suffering in the world.

It starts with self-love. Self-denial is not an option if we are to raise consciousness. The self is the gateway to Universal empowerment. So, when you deny the self, you are shutting the door to mass awakening. You are sending out the message that has gotten humanity so out of balance: that the self is not important.

This is the lie. The sense of humility that has been beaten into us all, has kept humanity enslaved. If those of goodness and kindness practice putting themselves below the rest, that allows for those of unethical means to take the helm. This is what we are experiencing now.

All those of goodness and light have to throw out the practice of self-sacrifice as it is taught. Self-abasement is a spiritual crime. Embrace your empowerment and yet see that same potential in everyone else. The ability to awaken ourselves and others has no dependence on outer issues.

The most depraved, underrated life can be a means of pulling all of humanity to the brink of awakening with their pure intention to do so and the purity of their love. When I was a child, I would grab onto any positive statement, song or event as evidence that being loving was a worthy cause.

Let us all give others a reason to be enthusiastic and hopeful about the possibilities of awakening. It is our most powerful healing tool. In this way, we ourselves are a divining rod for awakening.

COMPANIONSHIP

❧

ou Are the Magician, My Friend
Instead of thinking of everything in life as solid and a
blockage to work around, realize that all issues, feelings
and experiences are collapsible. Have you ever seen those collapsible
cups that a magician uses?

They can build them up very high. They can then flatten them
down to nothing by just pushing them down. It looks like magic. But
the cups are just collapsible. So is life. You can do it with all situations.

Everything we deal with in life has the same property. Even our
very atoms have the collapsible cup property. Feeling helpless, want,
need, hope, and even faith, lock the cups into a rigid stance. Enthusiasm, knowing, kindness, true integrity, communication and truth all
collapse the cups.

Think of the times you witnessed kindness breaking down the
walls in someone. This is collapsing the cups. Or when parties start
communicating and all the animosity between them got dissipated.
This is the cups being collapsed.

Miracles don't need to be so random. The cause does not need to
be so ominous. A miracle is someone tapping into the formula of how
to collapse the cups. The phrase, "doctors are calling it a miracle" can

be replaced with, "yet another individual figured out how to collapse the cups."

Maybe the thing that prevents miracles from striking in the same life twice is because the individual immediately gives thanks to an outer god rather than an inner Source. If you think about it, just switching the vantage point from God being somewhere in the sky to being an inner source of power is a form of collapsing the cups.

SENDING Prayers into the Cloud

Today, I witnessed a shift in consciousness. Everyone else may have overlooked it, but I was stunned by the simple sweetness of it. It was a snowstorm. All the traffic was moving around a truck that had its flashers on. It must not have had any snow tires on because it was slipping way more than necessary.

I watched from the vantage point of waiting to turn onto the highway from a side road. The truck was looming toward the inter-section at a very slow pace. There was a gap in the traffic. Then I saw this sweet gesture. I cried because I can imagine a world where everyone looks out for everyone else in this way. What I witnessed was a seed to a better world.

This HUGE salt truck and plow saw the truck struggling and did a U-turn. It turned itself around and moved in front of the truck. It plowed an already plowed road but threw down extra salt so the truck could gain some traction and maneuver.

It was then that I realized that kindness is noticing the things that others would dismiss and initializing an intention to address them. So, in a way, kindness is an intention to detail. So, when the Universe shows you something that others are overlooking, be grateful for your awareness.

Do whatever you are capable of doing to assist someone in a way that others are overlooking. It could be the Universe tapping you on the shoulder to fulfill a prayer. The truck that was swerving on the road was most likely praying for help. The plow truck answered his prayer with his assistance.

That is how prayers get answered. They get sent into the collective cloud and those who are tapped into their empowerment, or are open in the moment, will answer the prayer. The whole dynamic with asking and receiving prayer is the best version of social media that you will ever experience. God is an inside job. You are as important as you realize to be.

LIVING with the Grace of Gaia

This society lives with the reality of an unconscious fear that is written in the hearts of man. It affects all of our existence and is literally destroying the planet. The fear of man, one believes, is that woman will take man's power from him. But that is not the reality of the situation.

The true fear of man is not that woman will take his power from him. The true fear that lies innately in man is that woman will take HER power back from man. She had already given it over willingly a long time ago because women don't care about power. They care about love and pleasing everyone. Man wanted her power. So, she gave it willingly and graciously.

Think of the dynamics in many dysfunctional relationships. Female energy will give everything for those they love until there is nothing left of them. This is their nature. They will be happy to dilute themselves into nothing to better those they love. Unfortunately, we are seeing this play out in the world.

Female energy has diluted herself to the degree of almost extinction. The world is being parceled up in quarters by selfish, arrogant and imbalanced male energy. The affront to humanity has gotten so bad that mothers are being separated from their babies merely to create angst, which is a fuel source for power.

The desecration to Goddess was almost complete with such acts. It is Goddess' nature to give. But her giving unconditionally to male energy has created a warped and degenerative state of existence. Here is the crux of Gaia's dilemma: to truly give to all life, she must take back her power from man and create a balanced coexistence within the equilibrium of society.

This is difficult because of male energy and his belief that he is superior. It is also difficult because woman's nature to give has been exploited by man and has subjugated woman. Goddess must take back her empowerment without slipping into the denigration that male energy has operated. She must maintain her compassion, integrity, morality and sense of fairness as she usurps her rightful empowerment back from the maniacal hands of man.

Female energy must summon the strength to pull back the reins on male corruption. She does not do this because she craves power. She does this because she has compassion for all those who suffer under the thumb of man's rule.

She does not take back her power to sit on a dais and declare she is representing God. She takes back her power and redistributes it to the individuals that it was extracted from. All individuals must be emboldened to realize their worth and innate value. This is what is necessary for humanity to survive as a species.

Every lie that has been told to the masses was told by male energy to maintain power. The only lies that female energy has told are to herself. She is not weak. It takes more strength of character to maintain your integrity than to succumb to a brute. She is not insane or evil because she can see the beauty in all beings and can appreciate their true nature.

It is male energy that is stupid. It demonizes anything it doesn't understand and negates any truth that doesn't have his face at the center. He only listens to the best of male energy, and it is not to befriend him but to understand how to subjugate him until he destroys him. Male energy has become so warped and twisted that it has bled into the sacred vessel of the female body. It has created man-eaters out of some.

Male energy is no longer prominent in just men. Many women have become savvy in male energy. Taking, competing, besting others and ruthless practices are the handprint of male energy regardless of the genitals. In return, female energy has learned to hide by residing in the compassionate man as a means of survival.

We are obviously all meant to be a blend of both male and female energy. But there are some definite examples of prototypes of mostly male energy in men and women and mostly female energy in both male and female bodies.

The point is, no matter what your genitals define you as, it is time for all people to embrace more of female energy's qualities. Whether you are defined as male or female, it is time for you to embolden your compassionate side, speak to the injustices man accrues, see value in all life, give more than you take and love outside of your box of reason. Love with a desperation to see the weakest in life survive.

In loving as a compulsion, beyond all remnants of concern for how it is perceived; loving because it is your true nature and discerning truth by listening to your own innate wisdom, is embracing your female energy. It is taking something back from the clutches of power. It is living with the grace of Gaia.

SPACE TO GRIEVE

What happens in one's individual world is a reflection of what is happening Universally as well. The individual is the microcosm and the Universe is the macrocosm. Once you are able to make the correlation between the macrocosm and the microcosm, you seem to gain much wisdom because you can correlate your own experiences with those of the Universe.

When I was locked up, starving and enduring torture, I wasn't feeling sad. I didn't have the luxury of being sad. I was in survival mode. I had mind loops that I kept running in my head of, "how did I get in this situation?" and "how do I get free?" They consumed my energy. I did not feel sad or have any energy to waste on thoughts of self-pity.

I believe this is Universal. When I see animals suffering on different sites, in the time of their suffering, they are not feeling sorry for themselves. They are taking life in stride. It is only after they are free that they have the luxury of grieving the treatment that they received. They are not like people though in lamenting their past.

Animals have concerns about how long they will be able to have it so good after they are saved. The one question a rescued dog always asks their new people is, "How long do I get to stay this time?" But animals in general do not feel sorry for themselves. They will work out their issues in different ways, perhaps by being territorial or through their dreams.

You can tell when your pet is working out a trauma in their dreams because they wake up and look around like they don't recognize where they are. When you see them do this, this is a good time to cuddle with them and reassure them that they are in their forever home. They are safe, loved and a part of the family.

Humans are less apt to grieve when they are in survival mode. All their energy is allotted to surviving. There is a processing that happens after the danger subsides. When they are able to relax and feel safe, then the emotional aspect of their situation is able to process the trauma that they have endured.

This is true in the macrocosm as well. Humanity has been under assault for a very long time. For centuries there has been a domination of male energy that has enslaved all souls in an imbalance of cruelty, brutality and selfishness. But as female energy regains its footing to balance male energy, an end to the brutality can occur.

We have all been assaulted both as individuals and Universally. Collectively, all our energy has been allotted to being in survival mode. But, as more and more people awaken, there is a shift that is occurring. It is affording some of us the luxury to grieve for the collective. The grief is incredible. All the assaults on the collective include all the vulnerable, the deceived, manipulated, abused, those enduring the insanity of an assault and crimes against the most vulnerable of humanity.

Those of us who are sensitive cry easily. We are crying for the collective. We are crying for all those who are still assaulted and can't afford the luxury of grieving. Those who are depressed may be more tapped into the humanity of those who suffer. Those who are depressed may be sensing the plight of those who go hungry, are unloved, unwanted, assaulted and abused.

If someone is aware of the trials that happen outside of their own personal bubble, it may be confusing. In the present climate we have not been afforded the awareness to recognize our innate connection to others. So, our reactions may seem rogue. But the more that we awaken, the more we can recognize our incredible compassion for the plight of others.

In the "wake" of awakening, we can leave the solitary confinement of our own individualism and can roam more freely, experiencing the plight of our brethren. If you are feeling very sad or depressed, perhaps it is an occasion to rejoice. If you are aware enough to grieve pain with no discernible cause, perhaps you are awakening.

Perhaps you are exercising your legs of greater awareness. Perhaps you are simply starting to get a sense of your own omniscience. Perhaps the grief or depression that you are feeling is really a gauge to the depth of your own capacity to love.

The Dowry of Issues

I facilitated a private remote session with a woman whose husband was having issues. His reactions were extreme, and his boundaries were drawn in the sand. He was unhappy and making her unhappy. He was so caught up in his needs, fears and reactions that he was projecting them onto her and the marriage.

He wanted out of the marriage, he didn't want more kids, and he didn't want to be responsible in general. He was having strong reactions that didn't seem to show up earlier in the marriage. There were no red flags. In some instances, his stance and general amiability took a one hundred eighty-degree turn.

It seemed hopeless. But I always seem to get the answer. His reactions to their marriage seemed more to be in line with her parents' issues in a marriage. In probing deeper, the things she was struggling with or reacting to in the marriage were more like those of her in-laws. Her mother-in-law was more needy in their marriage. This very independent woman was feeling the issues of her mother-in-law as her own. Her husband was feeling the issues of her parents as his own.

So, what happens when two people commit in marriage is that they bring with them the engrams of their parents and merge them with their partner. Engrams are ingrained issues that are memories of past trauma. They play out in us and create habitual experiences that are not necessarily beneficial.

They are like the skip in a vinyl record that causes the song to repeat in one spot. The vinyl record would be your energy field; the scratch would be the emotional issue that gets played over and over again.

When we are in a family, we all combine our engrams, and so we are not only dealing with our issues but all those of every member. A child is brought up in the engrams of its parents and gets used to them. But when someone gets married, they now combine the engrams of their parents and their understanding of marriage from their point of view.

In this instance, the husband was having reactions to his in-laws' engrams that were brought to the marriage bed. They were not issues that he was immune to by growing up in them. His reactions were more like what his father-in-law was perceiving during his younger stint in marriage and not his own. In return, she was forced into reactions that were more like her mother-in-law's. This is how the unconscious dance commences.

Knowing the issue allows one to figure out the resolve.

(Say three times while tapping on your head and a fourth time while tapping on your chest.)

"I remove all of our parents' engrams of unhappiness from my marriage; in all moments."

"I remove all of our parents' engrams of fighting from my marriage; in all moments."

"I remove all of our parents' engrams of money issues from my marriage; in all moments."

"I remove all of our parents' engrams of immaturity from my marriage; in all moments."

You can continue the taps above but change out the issue each time with one of these:

Failure, lack of communication, neediness, addiction, dysfunction, restlessness, cheating, abuse, blame, control, sloppiness, anger, mental imbalance, selfishness, denial, rigidity, arrogance, disease, worry, suffering, etc.

THE FIRST LIFETIME *of Truth*

When you see the motive behind the corruption, the power mongers seem more pathetic than threatening. This awareness is the gateway to the evolution of higher consciousness through self-empowerment. The more you speak something, the more space that is created for it in this world.

That is why it is important to speak truth. Not as a means of bantering but as a means of transcending the attempts to bury consciousness in the rhetoric. What we do here is for future genera-tions. This is our time to shine and be a hero.

Complacency can live and die a million lifetimes. But truth etches itself in the ether and creates a foothold for humanity to expound.

MAKING *Portals*

The energy work that I do assists in all of humanity opening up to portals of possibility. It is such a pleasure to take profound metaphys-ical concepts and teach people how to empower themselves without their ever really realizing what drastic shifts are occurring.

When I say the world is geared for world peace, no one really believes it to the core. But what I am doing is opening a portal for world peace. It is similar to a technique the president uses to manifest something. But he does it for horrific causes that are to take democ-racy down and seat him in a position of world domination.

What he does is an instinctual abuse of power that has always worked for him. But what I am suggesting is for the good of all souls and an upgrade to the unconscious behavior we have all been swept up in. The world will advance to world peace. It is inevitable. And the shifts you are seeing in yourself, in your level of awareness and understanding, make it self-evident.

(Say each statement three times while tapping on your head and say it a fourth time while tapping on your chest.)

"We close all self-serving portals that trump opens; in all moments."

"We close all portals to suffering and dominion over others; in all moments."

"We close all portals that serve to empower trump; in all moments."

"We close all portals to all trump's ignoble intentions; in all moments."

"We close all portals to the self-serving alliance of dictators; in all moments."

"We close all portals to abuse of power; in all moments."

"We close all portals to being at the mercy of a madman; in all moments."

"We open all portals to accountability for all abusers of power; in all moments."

"We open all portals to self-reflection in regard to crimes against humanity; in all moments."

"We open all portals to individual Joy, Love, Abundance, Health and Freedom; in all moments."

"We open all portals to systemic ethical governing; in all moments."

"We open all portals to world peace; in all moments."

You Are Not Dying

That feeling that you are not going to be here long is a mind FU#k to keep you from putting out the intentions that you are capable. The only way the power mongering energy can thwart us is by trying to get people to shut down their own energy.

We are not able to be destroyed from without, so negativity tries to destroy us from within through our own thoughts. Now you know you can shift that and stop indulging that.

ENERGY ADJUSTMENT

Do you want to do some good?

(Say three times while tapping on your head and say it a fourth time while tapping on your chest.)

"We open all portals to our allies; in all moments."

"We close all portals to empowering dictators; in all moments."

"We open all portals to a path to citizenship; in all moments."

"We open all portals to repairing Puerto Rico; in all moments."

"We close all portals to tribalism; in all moments."

"We open all portals to nurturing the human spirit; in all moments."

"We close all portals to suffering; in all moments."

"We close all portals to trafficking; in all moments."

"We close all portals to demonizing conscious journalism; in all moments."

"We open all portals to individual freedoms; in all moments."

"We close all portals to demi-godding; in all moments."

"We close all portals to ignoble intentions; in all moments."

"We close all portals to fracking; in all moments."

"We close all portals created by lies; in all moments."

"We close all portals to global domination; in all moments."

"We open all portals to awakening; in all moments."

"We open all portals to individual freedoms; in all moments."

"We close all portals to primal conditioning; in all moments."

"We open all portals to self-discernment; in all moments."

"We close all portals to the desecration of the earth; in all moments."

"We open all portals to Universal Joy; in all moments."

"We close all portals that create human suffering; in all moments."

"We close all portals of hate; in all moments."

"We open all multifaceted portals of kindness; in all moments."

"We close all portals that induce fear; in all moments."

"We close all portals of poverty; in all moments."

"We close all portals to desecrating the earth; in all moments."

"We open all portals to honoring the wisdom of trees; in all moments."

"We open all portals valuing nature; in all moments."

"We close all portals to the worship of the rich; in all moments."

"We open all portals to Universal abundance; in all moments."

"We close all portals to mass incarceration; in all moments."

"We close all portals to mass enslavement; in all moments."

"We close all portals to systemic compartmentalization; in all moments."

"We open all portals to freedom; in all moments."

"We open all portals to integrity; in all moments."

"We open all portals to truth; in all moments."

"We close all portals to addiction; in all moments."

"We close all portals to the opioid crisis; in all moments."

"We close all malpractice abuse of western medicine and beliefs; in all moments."

"We open all portals to universal acceptance of natural healing; in all moments."

"We open all portals to optimal health; in all moments."

"We close all portals to being programmed to fail; in all moments."

"We close all portals to mental illness and dis-ease; in all moments."

"We close all portals to homelessness; in all moments."

"We open all portals to success; in all moments."

"We close all portals to having a madman in power; in all moments."

"We close all portals to enabling the madman in power; in all moments."

"We close all portals to the one life narrative used to enslave humanity; in all moments."

"We open all portals to the heavens; in all moments."

"We open all portals to understanding our past lives; in all moments."

"We close all portals to unworthiness; in all moments."

"We open all portals to mass awakening; in all moments."

"We open all portals to enlightenment; in all moments."

"We close all portals to the power mongers; in all moments."

"We open all portals to self-empowerment; in all moments."

IMPROVE *Your Experiences*

(Say each statement three times while tapping on your head and say it a fourth time while tapping on your chest.)

"I release experiencing sadness everywhere; in all moments."

"I release experiencing hate everywhere; in all moments."

"I release experiencing poverty everywhere; in all moments."

"I release experiencing slavery everywhere; in all moments."

"I release experiencing disease everywhere; in all moments."

"I release experiencing failure everywhere; in all moments."

"I release experiencing danger everywhere; in all moments."

"I release experiencing abandonment and rejection everywhere; in all moments."

"I release experiencing conformity everywhere; in all moments."

"I release experiencing war everywhere; in all moments."

"I release experiencing death everywhere; in all moments."

"I release experiencing fragmentation everywhere; in all moments."

"I release experiencing ugliness everywhere; in all moments."

"I release experiencing apathy and indifference everywhere; in all moments."

"I release experiencing discontent everywhere; in all moments."

"I release experiencing ignorance everywhere; in all moments."

"I release experiencing tribalism everywhere; in all moments."

"I release experiencing fear everywhere; in all moments."

"I release experiencing weakness everywhere; in all moments."

"I release experiencing cruelty everywhere; in all moments."

"I experience Joy everywhere; in all moments."
"I experience Love everywhere; in all moments."
"I experience Abundance everywhere; in all moments."
"I experience Freedom everywhere; in all moments."
"I experience Health everywhere; in all moments."
"I experience Success everywhere; in all moments."
"I experience Safety everywhere; in all moments."
"I experience Friendship everywhere; in all moments."
"I experience Creativity everywhere; in all moments."
"I experience Peace everywhere; in all moments."
"I experience Life everywhere; in all moments."
"I experience Wholeness everywhere; in all moments."
"I experience Beauty everywhere; in all moments."
"I experience Enthusiasm everywhere; in all moments."
"I experience Contentment everywhere; in all moments."
"I experience Spirituality everywhere; in all moments."
"I experience Enlightenment everywhere; in all moments."
"I experience Confidence everywhere; in all moments."
"I experience Strength everywhere; in all moments."
"I experience Compassion and Kindness everywhere; in all moments."
"I experience Integrity and Truth everywhere; in all moments."
"I experience Sincerity everywhere; in all moments."

THE HEALING POWER of *Teddy Bears*

Parents do their child a great disservice when they wean them off of their favorite plush toy. Their connection to their inanimate friend is very healing and empowering. There is a real nurturing nature to their relationship. The quality of your child's plush toys and their relationship with them is very important in your child's sense of security. Especially if they are a sensitive child.

I remember when I sensed a real dumbing down of the sensitivity and creativity in the world. It was a benchmark when I noticed plush toys became mass produced with little regard to the persona within them. Inanimate objects are made from living atoms. So, they have life force. They are alive.

When a group of atoms come together in a collective agreement, they form a group consciousness that is liken to a living intention, or a soul. The depth to the soul correlates to the depth of the sincerity of intention in creating the group consciousness. This intention shows up in quality of design, features, and structure.

There was a time when I noticed the life force diminish in the depth of the plush population. They had stupid, dull expressions on their faces with no enthusiasm or compassion. I am wondering now if, in some way, this was intentional to hinder the free will in humanity. But this was not the case for products made by certain companies. This is how companies like Disney started controlling the creative imagination of our children.

They understood this ability of plush toys and the imagination. They used them to create an Empire, driven and supported by the infinite untapped potential of a child's imagination. But the intention of breathing life into all the children's plush friends was just to lead them to the promised land of a theme park. Sure, some characters were beneficial to a child, but they always seemed programmed to whisper to the child the need to go to the theme parks. This may have been programmed into them. The plush toys were salesmen for the company.

It is similar to the action figures that are so popular. They are living companions and friends as far as the child is concerned. So many of them are programmed to fight and promote war. It is no wonder gun violence is so prevalent. So many children grow up on and are programed to accept violence through the toys that they are given as a child. This is no accident. Children are consciously being programmed through the intentions infused in the life of their toys. The more realistic, the better.

The whole Pokémon series is infused with the same psychic need as in the adult version of porn. Pokémon is pre-porn for children. They get addicted to the fervor and psychic energy of the brand and when they are older, the only thing that fills that wanton need is porn.

The craze for Pokémon easily transfers as a craze for porn. There is a strong desire to 'have more' infused in the Pokémon craze.

This is intentional to keep children enslaved to the fervor of spending. It is no matter to those who are making money if they are getting rich creating Pokémon characters or porn. This dark psychic energy is an example of what gets dried up in doing the SFT taps that I post. This is the kind of thing that you are addressing when doing the SFT taps.

These are all things for a parent to be aware of. When you bring a toy home to a child, you should be aware of the psychic intention of the objects. It is no different than wanting to know about the family of your children's friends to feel comfortable that they are safe.

There are many well-made toys that have the intention of nurturing the child and making them feel safe. To a sensitive child, the toys around them are real. If they have an initial response not to like a toy, please don't make them warm up to them. They are sensitive to the intentions of the plush toys you introduce them to. A safe bet is to give them plush toys that realistically depict animals in nature. These stuffed animals will actually enhance their compassion for wildlife.

Try to find one good friend for your child. One that has features that are compassionate, strong, caring and nurturing. The reason the Care Bears were called Care Bears was to be nurturing for the child. But their expression and aptitude were limited. A child can be comforted by a plush companion that is wiser than they are. Plush beings that present themselves as a similar age and experience of your child may be too limiting a comfort for your child.

The best friend plush toy of your child can be very healing. Adults like to complain and vent to dissipate all the angst that they have collected. Children collect angst and don't process it as easily. Their brain is not formed to articulate the bombardment of negativity that they are experiencing. Angst can just stay dormant in a child in a pool of confusing energy unless they can pass it off.

When they are older, they can pass it through healthy communication, play and exercise. Being in nature also help pass off the excess energy. Another way to dissipate the feelings and thoughts of the day is for the child to pass them off to their plush friend.

Energy transfer through inanimate objects is a great form of healing. That is how rocks and crystals are healing. They absorb negative energy and release the logjam of negative energies that are preventing the energy system of the individual from rejuvenating itself. When a child hugs their teddy bear, they are releasing all the angst in them into the inanimate world. It is neutralized there, and the child is replenished.

This works for adults as well. Remember the adage to become as little children to seek the kingdom of heaven? This is one way. If you find the right plush companion, it can take you to a safe and nurturing experience. This is a great technique for energy workers to adopt and for those who don't allow just anyone to do work on them. Also, a great technique for any caregiver or even one with fibromyalgia.

Any person who is so filled up with issues from caring too much or being overwhelmed by life, would do well to pass all their angst into a caring teddy bear through a hug. It sounds ridiculous and yet this is a harmless practice that can bring so much calm to so many. Are you brave enough to be vulnerable in this way? Try it as a form of self-healing. Choose a friend wisely and keep them for life.

CREATIVITY

efinitions
It is great to wake up to someone who is truly happy to see you. That is why there are cat ladies.

It is great to be around and appreciate someone who truly gives all of themselves unconditionally. That is why there are tree huggers.

It is great to be treated by a healer who doesn't write you off as terminal. That is why we have alternative medicine.

It is great to have such an understanding of the nature of life that you don't totally disconnect from anyone who is dead. That is why there are spiritualists.

It is great to be able to experience the omnipotence of one's own empowerment and be willing to deal with the reality of the limitations of this existence as payment for that awareness. That is what is called bi-polar.

It is great to be able to perceive in energy beyond the limitations of the written symbol yet spend your whole life feeling inadequate for doing so. That is what it is to be dyslexic.

It is great to be aware enough to perceive life beyond the insanity of the current societal rules yet without the benefit of an understanding of one's own empowerment. That is what is called mental illness.

It is great to remember our past experiences of being either male or female so fondly that they register beyond our current class stamping system of genital identification. This is called being gay.

It is great to be so comfortable in one's skin and have a fondness for both experiences of being either male or female that one can move fluently through life without being compartmentalized into either male or female. This is called being transgender.

It is great to be so fed up with the rules of the slave masters that hold people trapped in the conveyor belt existence of a "nine-to five" reality that one bows out entirely just to be free. This is why there are so many homeless.

It is great to honor and respect God in all forms of life as opposed to the arrogant notion that God looks only like us in male form. That is why there are pagans.

There is a desperate need to live in in a place where one is totally accepted exactly as they are. That is why there are nature lovers.

It is great to be able to create the world that you are a part of beyond the physical skin. That is why we have dreams.

It is great to be able to take the understanding that we acquire in our dreams and manifest as much of it as possible here on earth. That is why there is imagination and creativity.

It is great to get a sense of all the experiences one has ever had happen being playing out in real time in others and relating to them without feeling the anguish too deeply. That is what is called compassion.

It is great to strive to rectify all the wrongs that have ever been afflicted on humanity using the current warped system. This is what it is called democratic socialism.

It is great to use our present talents to rectify all the wrongs that have ever happened to us and that we have ever inflicted on others. This is what our purpose is.

It is great to see the world living in its purpose beyond the pettiness of judgment; to uplift all life as a reflection of their true nature. This is world peace.

THE MODERN MYSTIC

When the Bible was first written, Christianity was not an established religion. In fact, the Bible is a compilation of experiences of mystics who had forged their own way to enlightenment. The Bible is a collection of their experiences. Religion, in a way, has become the lowest common denominator of the mystic's experiences.

The mystics didn't follow an outer mandate. They listened to their inner promptings to connect to Source from within. Their passion, devotion and resilience were documented and packaged in a way that worked against most readers duplicating their spiritual progress.

The irony is that people who follow the Bible seem to be more likely to demonize the modern mystic. The modern mystic doesn't need to follow a group's agenda. In fact, they are more likely to have outgrown the doctrine in any book or group.

The modern mystic most likely loves nature, appreciates the wisdom of trees, embraces the truth in music, art and poetry. They may have lost their voice because of memories of genocide by those who worked to squelch truth. But their inner light and unique view of life is apparent to others. Those who are awakening gravitate to them. Those who are still sleeping will resent them.

There are factions working today to squelch truth. The have always worked to squelch truth. They work to divide us and keep humans trapped in primal mode. But more mystics are regaining their inner empowerment to assist all souls in awakening. The job of the mystic is to follow their inner mandate to truth. They know that the Source of all light, love and truth is within, and they strive diligently to forge a path for all others to find truth within as well.

If you are reading this, you are most likely a mystic and are feeling the gratitude of not having to go it quite alone anymore. We all assist in Light and Love to awaken those who suffer in ignorance and despair. Thank you for your service to humanity. You and it are priceless.

Meeting in the Middle

The left is closer to the middle than it is being depicted; there are factions trying to prevent humanity from evolving. It is trying to pull all of society back hundreds of years to keep us all enslaved to outmoded issues. Naturally evolving fossil fuel, white supremacy, and women's issues are not extreme. They are natural. As natural as love.

If you watch an event and get a twinge of fear because there are less and less white faces in the crowd, challenge those feelings as irrational. It is harboring the primal vibration that is being stoked to ignite hate. What we hold in our personal orbit is magnified in the collective.

Please realize that we all have experienced lives with every color skin and every human condition under the sun. The more we can access our own oppression from past lives, the more we can adopt incredible compassion for anyone who is slighted in any way in this life.

It is those who are trapped in the belief of one-life that are more apt to judge in fear of losing what they presently have. Perhaps it is time to express more freely our understanding of and experiences with our past lives. Perhaps the easing of the one-lifers into an understanding of their own immortality is the peripheral way to coax hate, prejudice and dependence on fossil fuel out of their clutched hands.

Closing Your Energy

In the old days, people understood the dynamics of energy. Prayer was a means to open your energy up in an expansive way to an expansive message. After the opening, there needed to be a way to close your energy back down to stay protected.

The phrase Amen is not meant as a statement of agreement. It is a means to close the aura down after it has expanded. But people are too closed. They don't need to close down their energy any more than it is. They need to expand it as much as possible.

When I write something, its purpose is to open the reader up to more truth. The reader may not understand the dynamic but may feel it. When they respond to the message by saying "amen," they are closing their energy down.

It is just an observation to be aware of. Saying Amen is a means to close the energy field down. If this is your intention, great. If you want to stay open, you may want to change this expression.

Let the Tears Flow

Some people have not been able to cry. Here are taps to assist in releasing the tears.

(Say three times while tapping on your head and say a fourth time while tapping on your chest.)

"I release being numb with pain; in all moments."

"I release the fear of emoting; in all moments."

"I release confusing tears with vulnerability; in all moments."

"I release holding back the tears; in all moments."

"I release associating crying with giving my abuser satisfaction; in all moments."

"I release shutting down to prove I am strong; in all moments."

"I release holding the pain within; in all moments."

"I release holding back the tears as a 'fuck you' to the abuser; in all moments."

"I release being milked of all my emotion; in all moments."

"I reclaim my right to grieve; in all moments."

"I release being pushed over the edge; in all moments."

"I release the fear that tears will take me over the edge; in all moments."

"I release losing everything but my tears; in all moments."

"I release confusing crying with giving up; in all moments."

"I release confusing crying with surrendering to the enemy; in all moments."

"I release confusing tears as the last vestige before death; in all moments."

"I release the trauma of death looming near; in all moments."

"I release confusing tears with death; in all moments."

"I remove all threats to not cry; in all moments."

"I remove all curses to not be able to cry; in all moments."

"I allow the flood of tears to flow; in all moments."

"I heal myself through my tears; in all moments."

"I nurture myself through my tears; in all moments."

"I love myself through my tears; in all moments."

"I balance myself through my tears; in all moments."

"I give myself permission to cry; in all moments."

"I unleash all the endorphins associated with crying; in all moments."

"I exonerate myself; in all moments."

YOU AND TRUTH

Truth is not public opinion

Truth is not based on who can bury their sins better

Truth is not buying up the media to slant the story

Truth is not at the mercy of professional liars

It is not spun and distorted to protect a bloated liar.

TRUTH DOES NOT NEED you to be polished up pretty

It is organic

It seeps into the skin like a rich lotion

Truth does not leave so many questions

It does not have an agenda.

TRUTH DOES NOT LINE the pockets of the rich

It does not create division

Truth does not need repetition to be received

It doesn't need to be coerced into the psyche
Truth is not giving candy and presents to children on sacred days
to bribe their devotion.
Truth creates a connection to your own depth
The place in you that knows all the answers
It is a self-reliance that doesn't need prompting to understand
It sees the distortion in the liars
It sees how hard the psychic waves are working to prevent the
world from awakening.

TRUTH HAS BEEN SQUELCHED for so long that the lies have become
friends
They are the dust bunnies that collect around the truth
They are more apparent than the truth
And more welcome
They propagate at will to prevent truth from prevailing.

LIES WILL COAX, bribe and reassure you in any way possible
They will do anything to keep you distracted from truth
They will induce fear, threaten and even rape you of your dignity
Anything that the most heinous crimes can offer, so too can the
lies.

YOUR DENIAL IS the prize
Your demonizing of the truth is the goal
Your staying happy in your defenses and reprimand of the truth
are vital.
You attack truth effortlessly
In blissful ignorance.

EVERY TIME you judge others

Every time you forgo speaking your truth out of niceties
Every time you birth another opinion based on arbitrary facts
Every time you go along with the crowd
And become complacent to your own potential.

You ARE the pinnacle factor whether the world awakens or lays in
greed until its own destruction
You are the factor whether all souls see their worth
Or bow to a sniffling power monger
Your seeing your own worth and potential encourages all others to
do the same.

You ARE the saint or sinner you deem yourself to be
Groveling in unworthiness only emboldens the unworthy to rule
Why do you care so little about others?
Why do you not just embrace your omnipotence?
Why do you not challenge the shackles that tell you that you are
insignificant?

IF YOU VALUE GOD, you must value yourself
You must listen to what your heart tells you
The part of the heart not programmed by the mind
Think, feel, discern into truth unfettered by fear or opinions
Bleed your love into the collective so that all can awaken from the
lies.

You ARE pinnacle
Your essence coaxes truth to the surface in others
You are a portal of truth in this world
You can melt the ice of fear and indifference
You are the golden child to the awakening of truth.

The sun rises and sets on you
You matter.

STOP WASTING *Energy*

(Say each statement three times while tapping on your head and say it a fourth time while tapping on your chest.)

"I convert all the energy of self-derision into kinetic energy for empowerment; in all moments."

"I convert all the energy of apathy into kinetic energy for empowerment; in all moments."

"I convert all the energy of mind fucks into kinetic energy for empowerment; in all moments."

"I convert all the energy of psychic illusion into kinetic energy for empowerment; in all moments."

"I convert all the energy of indecision into kinetic energy for empowerment; in all moments."

"I convert all the energy of fear into kinetic energy for empowerment; in all moments."

"I convert all the energy of in-fighting into kinetic energy for empowerment; in all moments."

"I convert all the energy of degenerating into kinetic energy for empowerment; in all moments."

"I convert all the energy of slowing down into kinetic energy for empowerment; in all moments."

"I convert all the energy of male dominance into kinetic energy for empowerment; in all moments."

"I convert all the energy of pulling back engrams into kinetic energy for empowerment; in all moments."

"I convert all the energy of senseless talk into kinetic energy for empowerment; in all moments."

"I convert all the energy of mind loops into kinetic energy for empowerment; in all moments."

"I convert all the energy of time and space entrapment into kinetic energy for empowerment; in all moments."

. . .

ENCOURAGEMENT AND UNDERSTANDING

Looking backwards is a habitual coping method. It is like looking behind you when you are running for your life. Change will happen more easily if people will stop comparing the future to the past. The world has evolved beyond the limitations of what has already occurred. People need to understand that the linear political past cannot affect the exponential political future.

If you want to support change in the world, stop reverting to old fear patterns set up by those in control to maintain control. Be as idealistic and expansive in your hopes for the future as a child awaiting a magical windfall on Christmas morning.

This is the passion and enthusiasm necessary to propel humanity into the realms of Joy, Love, Abundance, Freedom and Peace. It is the last push in the birthing process. Don't allow the muscle memory of discouragement to dampen your enthusiasm for a greater outcome.

Let's face it; we were all deceived. But let's not let the facade of the smug veneer prevent us from collecting our gifts, honing our crafts, and gifting the world with our greatness. The synergy of our intentions creates a new outcome never seen by man. It will be inevitable to awaken. Ignorance will die and so will the rusted ways of greed and discontent.

The future of the next day brings exponential new awareness. So, don't inflict it with the fear of yesterday. Our governing system will reflect our new awakening. Our integrity, strength, compassion and kindness will usher in a new day. Be confident in what your heart, gut and instincts tell you and expound that confidence outward.

We have got this. All the rhetoric and apathy in the world cannot deny this truth. We are expounding in all moments. Godspeed.

CHANGING THE ALGORITHMS
OF LIFE

∽

The Consciousness of Inanimate Objects

Objects have consciousness. They are infused with an intention when they are created. They have an identity and wish to be validated. They may not have an individual mind, but they are created under the confines of the Universal Mind.

And though humans negate their individual identity, inanimate objects still have a consciousness. Meaning, on some level, they know for what purpose they were created. As with any other soul, they desire to be useful. They desire to fulfill the intention for which they were created.

For example, a sweet baby doll or teddy bear will entice a child to love and hold them. This draw is so strong that it can entice an adult to cuddle it as well. Those more sensitive to perceiving in energy, like some women, will be drawn to the energy of a teddy bear. That is why teddy bears can be used to entice a woman to fall in love, along with flowers and chocolate. A similar enticement is innate in a cute hand-bag, hat, makeup, or car.

In fact, it is a billion-dollar industry to infuse a beckoning energy into such items so that the vulnerable buyer will be drawn to a partic-ular item more than another. The items created are infused with a

psychic energy beckoning for them to be bought and, more impor-
tantly, to be used.

No one buys a car to have it sit in the driveway. The commercials
always show it being driven to the edge of the earth. The car or truck
promises to bring you adventure, fun and freedom. It is not the truck
alone you are buying, but the promise of a greater version of yourself
that is infused in the packaging of the item.

The same is true with guns. Guns know what their purpose is.
They don't have a consciousness as far as right or wrong. But there is
an enticement that is part of them that beckons them to be used. So, if
people buy a gun just to have it in the house for protection, know that
the gun itself will attract the opportunities to it to be used.

Since this world is so hot triggered for negativity, a negative intention may override a positive intention of the same vibration. Meaning
that the innocent intention to have a gun on your person may be
overridden by the gun's intention to be used. This may account for
why so many accidental deaths happen with a gun that was never
meant to be used.

The whole concept of gun control is thwarted from the way it is
being looked at. Those who sell guns want to keep the issue immersed
in the realms of fear. When there is fear around an issue, people maintain a reactionary mode or primal mode. When people are in primal
mode, there is an inability to discern facts and truth.

There is so much psychic energy around guns, the issue of guns,
and those who govern from a corrupt point of view. All this entangle-
ment has made it difficult for individuals to discern for themselves.
When someone is in a hypersensitive state, they are more apt to
perceive in energy without the understanding of what is happening.

When someone perceives in energy, they are more apt to hear and
react to the beckoning of an item that is compelling them to use it.
Semi-automatic guns were made to gun people down. This is their
purpose. So, when one is more susceptible to buy something like this,
they are also more susceptible to listen to its desire to be used.

It is short-sighted and self-serving to allow these items to be made.
The original intention should never have been allowed to be formu-

lated. Instead of scapegoating those more apt to perceive in energy by demonizing them as mentally ill, we should all learn to perceive in energy, so we understand the true dynamics at play.

WITH TWO LOAVES of Bread

Jesus said in his day, what I do, you can do and more. It is true. Those of us who understand the dynamics of healing and the interplay of energy are able to assist in the suffering of man more than is realized.

Jesus fed a crowd of people with two loaves of bread. It was a matter of tapping into the energy of nourishment and infusing the experience into the needy. We can do the same on a larger scale. There are people suffering at the hands of cruelty.

It may seem silly to even try this exercise. But the alternative is to know the multitudes are being tortured through lack of sustenance. If there is a possibility that some of you will claim your empowerment and assist in this way, then it could be deemed a miracle.

A miracle is embracing possibilities before they are universally accepted. At one point, flying, computers and medicine would have been considered miracles.

(Say three times while tapping on your head and say a fourth time while tapping on your chest.)

"We infuse the vibration of nourishment, sustenance, satisfaction and kindness into all those who are being starved; in all moments."

"We usurp all those who starve the masses; in all moments."

"We abolition the practice of starving the masses; in all moments."

"We eliminate the first cause in starving the masses; in all moments."

"We starve out ruthlessness and cruelty; in all moments."

"We infuse nourishment and sustenance into all individuals of the collective; in all moments."

"We infuse nourishment and sustenance into the universal sound frequency; in all moments."

"We imbue nourishment and sustenance into the universal light emanation; in all moments."

"We are centered and empowered in universal nourishment and sustenance; in all moments."

"We resonate, emanate and are interconnected with all life in universal nourishment and sustenance; in all moments."

THE GREEN NEW DEAL

The Green New Deal is the intention of becoming a hundred percent sustainable energy in ten years. It is so exciting to see such progressive agendas even being talked about in political circles.

This is evidence of the work we do with the taps. The work we do here is literally paving a way for higher consciousness. We are dissipating psychic walls and chains of manipulation, illusion and fear. These are dynamic times as we all are awakened to our empowerment, which is a by-product of the incredible work we do here.

Please continue to do the taps. In past times, it sometimes took only one individual with a vision to drive humanity to betterment through change. We who do the taps are creating a synergy of our dynamic efforts and are witnessing the blossoming of enlightenment through our efforts.

(Say three times while tapping on your head and say it a fourth time while tapping on your chest.)

"We make space in this world for the Universal acceptance of the Green New Deal; in all moments."

"We remove all blockages to the Universal acceptance of the Green New Deal; in all moments."

"We open all portals to the Universal acceptance of the Green New Deal; in all moments."

"We remove all limitations on the Universal acceptance of the Green New Deal; in all moments."

"We stretch our capacity to Universally accept the Green New Deal; in all moments."

"We are centered and empowered in the Universal acceptance of the Green New Deal; in all moments."
"We resonate, emanate and are interconnected to all life in the Universal acceptance of the Green New Deal; in all moments."

REVELATIONS

The end of the world, as predicted, is actually the end of linear existence and being trapped in the third dimension. The end of the world is actually the transcendence to the fifth dimension. We are living out the Book of Revelations and the four horsemen are the dictators that have tried to band together to enslave humanity.

The plague that is mentioned that covers the world is apathy. The work I do is to dry up the apathy and psychic control and assist all souls to regain their empowerment and awaken. We are experiencing the shift and it is dynamic and empowering.

CHANGING *the Algorithms of Life*

This morning I posted a new message called Avoiding War. The truths I put in that post were new concepts that I have never shared before. I posted it on one of my pages and I was going to share it on my group page. But after I posted the post, my server would not work.

I could not get my e-mails and my social media pages to work. The computer went haywire. I couldn't even connect via phone with a group session I was slated to facilitate. Some of you may experience this when you share positive posts, causing your page to malfunction. It seems like a coincidence, right? It is not. It happens all the time to me.

The reason this happens is because the world of illusion that we live in does not accept truth in its present algorithm. When I post something with truth in it, it has to be accepted because I am a product of this illusion because I live here. The algorithm that doesn't accept truth tried to prevent me from getting to the point of sharing truth. But it failed. I am here. I exist here but am not really of this world. I exist on the peripheral of life to do the work that I do.

The post that I posted on avoiding war was accepted and eventually my page started to work. The truth of my post is accepted into existence, but most people will not notice it. This is because the algorithm of truth is not very high on the priorities of life. Truth is begrudgingly allowed. But it is met also with the algorithms to ignore truth, disbelieve truth, discredit truth or find it inconvenient to do anything about it.

But still, here we are sharing truth. So, here is an invitation for you to use your abilities to change the algorithms of life. Do the Energetic Cleanse on the negative issues of the world that you want to see have less grip on humanity. This work is very deep. See the Energetic Cleanse in Chapter 13 and do the exercise on the following issues.

- Algorithms of war
- Algorithms of corruption
- Algorithms of western medicine
- Algorithms of male dominance
- Algorithms of mass incarceration
- Algorithms of white supremacy
- Algorithms of oligarchies
- Algorithms of dictatorships
- Algorithms of pollution
- Algorithms of dark money
- Algorithms of ignorance
- Algorithms of tribalism
- Algorithms of the Dark Ages
- Algorithms of political control
- Algorithms of religious control
- Algorithms of slavery
- Algorithms of poverty
- Algorithms of disease
- Algorithms of entitlement
- Algorithms of unequal dispersion of wealth

- Algorithms of hate
- Algorithms of linear enslavement
- Algorithms of lies
- Algorithms of desecrating earth
- Algorithms of mass gun use
- Algorithms of fossil fuels
- Algorithms of a one-life narrative
- Algorithms of trafficking

You will be using your empowerment as a programmer of Life. The more that people do this, the more space will be freed up for truth, love, joy and other things of empowerment.

YOUR OWN TRIGGERS

Whenever you are presented with information of any kind, whether media, friends or hearsay, pay attention to how it is received in your body and energy. You control what you allow in. So many people politely allow themselves to be subjected to a bombardment of negativity out of the premise of being nice. When did we become a society of victims and martyrs?

When you are receiving new information, pay attention to how your body receives it. Are you being goaded into anger, fear or to shut down further and say, "it will work out?" Being complacent in how you experience life may be preventing you from being the dynamic version of yourself that you truly are.

People ask me all the time when I realized that I had special talents in healing and in moving energy. It happened when I stopped agreeing with everyone who diminished me. I stopped beating them to the punch and putting myself down before they had a chance to. Self-derision was my way of saying that I knew what they thought of me and I am smart enough to see it before they point it out. It was definitely a defeatist attitude and betrayed the only person that truly has my back, me.

When you forgo the self-derision and the negative banter; when you refuse to agree with the niceties of how messed up the world is; when you refuse to allow yourself to be a dumping ground for other people's toxic buildup; and when you refuse to be manipulated into the primal reactionary modes of hate or fear, you will make space in your energy system to allow a little gratitude in for what a dynamic, complex being you really are.

Gratitude literally opens up all the energy systems of your body. Fear, hate, worry and regret shut down your energy system. When you are in fear, hate or regret, you are locked in your physical body and cut off from access to all the truth and wisdom of the Universe that a more grateful energy system has access to.

Gratitude allows you the space in your own orbit to be comfortable maintaining your physicality while retrieving the answers to all that you wish to know. If you ask the Universe any question, it will supply you the answers that you seek. But you need to remain open to the answers by not allowing yourself to be locked in a sarcophagus of fear, hate or pain.

Any issue can be released from the body. You adopt the vantage point of a more spacious awareness of yourself if you choose. Instead of seeing yourself as the dead weight of a body, see yourself at the vantage point of being a galaxy. From that point of view, you can see the energy of the physical body as more fluid and resilient. From that vantage point you can have more of an impact on the releasing of stagnant energy that you process as pain or emotional issues, rather than when you are looking at them trapped inside the body.

If you are trapped in the body, pain and emotional issues seem larger than life. If you are looking at the same issues from the vantage point of being a galaxy, the issues are much smaller and easier to dissipate. When I work as the healer to release stagnant energy from others, I am always doing it from the vantage point of a galaxy.

That is why the concept of taking on karma is obsolete. How can a galaxy take on anything from such a minimal source? The whole dynamic of healing will change as everyone realizes themselves as the dynamic galaxy that they are.

From the vantage point of a galaxy, it's easy to dissipate the stagnant energy that has collected in any one body. Recently, I was facilitating a remote private session and I was using my abilities in remote viewing and medical intuitiveness to discover a deeper secret in regard to healing.

It really isn't a secret, but it is a truth hidden in plain sight. Humans have been conditioned to stay locked in the body so that all the realizations that they could be enjoying seem like they are hidden. But it is all those in the human condition that have shut their eyes to them.

Would you keep your eyes shut and refuse to look at the world if someone asked you to? In a sense, you have shut down incredible perceptions out of fear and conditioning. What I write is a means to coax you to open up your spiritual eyes. Open up your subtle senses and partake of truth.

In this remote session, I saw that the stagnant energy that I release from a body to make it well had another layer to release, that could maybe assist those struggling with a hardwired diagnosis. I looked deeper into a particular body and scrutinized all the cells. They were like clear, little globes that were all tainted each on the same side with the tartar buildup of stagnant energy. They looked like blown or sooty bulbs--all on the same one side.

I used this information to formulate an intention in the form of a visualization to see myself from the vantage point of the galaxy, as stretching the body out to create space and movement. I visualized undulating the body like a piece of fabric I was washing in a tub of water, except it was in the spaciousness of a galaxy; that was the cleansing agent. It was a means to loosen all the tartar that was in each individual globe which represented individual cells of the body.

As I did this, the client on the other end of the phone call could perceive what I was doing and could sense her body relaxing and releasing. She gained more clarity and peace of mind as I continued. I went through the different areas of her body that had more tartar buildup of stagnant emotional issues that stained her cells.

Her head showed places in it that stored more buildup. This showed up as stubbornness in her life. Her heart was fine, but what I saw in her head was similar to what I have seen in other people's hearts as plaque in the arteries. The stagnant energy created plaque in the cells of her head just like it creates plaque in other's hearts. The plaque buildup in their arterial walls is stagnant energy deposited for years. This plaque was revealing a truth to the way all cells process energy and store emotional issues.

We went through the whole body to cleanse all the cells of the emotional tartar that had built up in them and would at some point interfere with their normal function and perhaps have initiated a disease in the body.

This process was a profound discovery to me that would have gone unrealized if I still engaged in self-defacing attacks, being manipulated by rhetoric or fear and allowed myself to be a dumping ground for someone else who has locked themselves in a very small reality of pain and problems. As I write this, I am wondering what truths you are awaiting to discover and share? What are they? The world is waiting.

Clear Your Brain Fog

The whole concept of a smoking gun is nailing in the misnomer that we can't think for ourselves; that we must have all the details of an intention laid at our feet until we can act. We are being paralyzed into inaction by this concept.

What is playing out in society at large is also playing out in our own personal lives. These taps will assist us all. They will also assist all of humanity to accept the truth of the actions that are playing out.

The world is desperate for us to assist them in awakening.

(Say three times while tapping on your head and say them a fourth times while tapping on your chest.)

"I declare myself a surrogate for humanity in doing these taps; in all moments."

"I release the disconnect between cause and effect; in all moments."

"I release disregarding the effects of obvious causes; in all moments."

"I release filtering out the effect of obvious causes; in all moments."

"I release the need to be bombarded by a series of effects to validate the initial cause; in all moments."

"I recognize the effect as readily as I acknowledge the cause; in all moments."

"I strengthen the synapses between cause and effect; in all moments."

"I dissipate all psychic energy that prevents me from acknowledging the effects of all causes; in all moments."

"I strip away all illusions that hide the effects of all causes; in all moments."

"I dissipate the psychic energy that highlights alternative facts as reality; in all moments."

"I release being hypnotized or manipulated into believing in alternative facts; in all moments."

"I am impervious to being programmed by repetition; in all moments."

"I release ascribing outer sources as a source for truth; in all moments."

"I release believing outer sources over my own compass; in all moments."

"I release deferring to an outer agenda; in all moments."

"I release being immersed in apathy by refusing to acknowledge truth; in all moments."

"I release the fear of acknowledging all the effects of all causes; in all moments."

"I release being deduced to a mental stupor; in all moments."

"I release being paralyzed in inaction; in all moments."

"I release the fear of being wrong; in all moments."

"I release being ostracized for speaking truth; in all moments."

"I release being tortured or killed for speaking truth; in all moments."

"I release the need to be polite in refusing to address an initial wrong; in all moments."

"I release doubting myself; in all moments."

"I release turning my integrity into mush; in all moments."

"I release confusing strength for anger; in all moments."

"I access my strength without engaging in anger; in all moments."

"I release burying my truth and causing disease; in all moments."

"I maintain my outer calm without dipping into apathy; in all moments."

"I eliminate the first cause in the disconnect between each cause and each effect; in all moments."

"I strengthen the conviction in acknowledging the effect of each cause; in all moments."

"I release being so easily conditioned; in all moments."

"I shift my paradigm from being conditioned to knowing truth; in all moments."

"I embrace the randomity of truth; in all moments."

"I hard wire the true effects to all causes; in all moments."

"I trust my ability to discern truth; in all moments."

"I scrutinize all outer facts and sources against the master truth of my own inner compass; in all moments."

"I am centered and empowered and confidently discerning truth; in all moments."

"I release being closed off to truth; in all moments."

"I stay perpetually open to realizing more truth; in all moments."

"I disregard all lies that I accepted as truth; in all moments."

"I undo the programming and conditioning of all lies; in all moments."

"I resonate, emanate and am interconnected with all life in confidently discerning truth; in all moments."

"I am a portal of truth; in all moments."

"All lies dissipate in my wake; in all moments."

"I am awakened; in all moments."

How to Dry Up Psychic Energy

There is a residual energy that is created through thoughts and feelings. It is a somewhat murky energy that collects around living beings. Some people get pretty slimy. At a certain point, this energy starts to identify with the person it is around or with others that it is subjected to. It starts to react as if they were the same; the way jello will react if its container is moved.

This personification of energy is what people have been taught to believe as entities or even evil spirits. The thing about this energy is that it grows by having a strong reaction to it. Being afraid of it feeds it. So does adding thought energy to it by thinking of it. Obsessing over it is the best thing you can do to intensify the experience of it.

The best thing you can do if something is causing you distress is to withdraw all your attention from it. Humans still don't realize what a driving force their own intentions are, especially if they are driven by fear. Harnessing people's fear is the way the power factions stay in control. It has become such a parlor trick at this point that, to some of us, it is absurd that people still fall for it.

These psychic energies can be addressed by anyone who practices the art of operating in a pure state of concentrated love. Concentrated love is not a peppy over-the-top state. That kind of love is channeled through the hormonal system and is like a sugar rush. Concentrated love is a still calmness that the individual exudes. It can be intimidating. It is as intimidating as stark truth.

Some people experience this when they encounter someone who makes them feel uncomfortable in their skin just by their presence. The reason that they are feeling uncomfortable is that some of the psychic energies that collect on someone and fortify their ego are being stripped away through the mere presence of love and truth in the intimidating person's countenance.

One can develop this cleansing agent of psychic energy through personal discipline. It involves learning NOT to react under any situation. Reactions are the way psychic energy is created. So, by forgoing reacting, one is able to stay more present to the reality at hand instead of being swept into psychic manipulation.

Non-reaction happens when one can refrain from judging anything that they are introduced to. Refrain from fear, hate and outrage. Try not to snap in a reactionary mode of taking action either.

This prevents you from separating yourself from the psychic energies at hand.

Even if you are not being outwardly swayed in the moment, by kneejerk reacting you are immersing yourself in the psychic energies and making it more difficult to get free from them. I know people who have galvanized themselves in theses energies. It is more difficult to free yourselves of these energies when you think they are an aspect of you.

That is why getting your feelings hurt is not really a bad thing. If you have any intentions to be an awakened spiritual being, you will get your feelings hurt all the time. You will even feel targeted because to be crushed and to feel lost and demoralized seem to be your main-stay. This is the Universe intentionally lobbing these psychic energies off of you.

Having your feelings hurt is always a good thing in spiritual terms. The feeling bad is the raw skin of the real you being exposed. It is no different than when a crusty scab falls off and the new skin under-neath feels vulnerable. When you are around someone who is awak-ened, these crusty energy scabs are going to be ripped off. It doesn't feel good unless the person can identify with their empowered-self and embrace the process.

The ability to dissipate the psychic energies can be developed through practice. It is done by holding a stance of a loving state unen-cumbered by thoughts or feelings. Society will try to motivate you into reaction by showing you an appalling image and daring you not to react.

This happens a lot with social media through showing abused animals, despicable crimes or hated political figures. The reader does not realize that they are being goaded into reacting as fuel for the very causes they detest the most. By not reacting and staying in a place of concentrated love, you do more for abused animals everywhere than sharing the image in outrage.

Sure, you can act to affect change. Just act, not react. When you act because you were introduced to some stimuli, you are being a pawn for the intention of another. If you stay in a stance of non-reaction and concentrated love, then you know that every time you act, it is to empower others, not to enslave them.

I was walking in the grocery store and came next to a very tall woman who didn't strike me as attractive. I didn't have an opinion, but as I got around her, I could hear all the insults people had encapsulated her in with their thoughts. I heard them all. If I were less aware, I would have thought they were my own thoughts. But they weren't. They were the buildup of other people's judgments that had built up on her.

It was my automatic response to strip away this ugly psychic energy that she was walking around with. It is quite easy for me to do. I simply introduce my loving intention for them to be free of the energy into manifestation. My love is like caustic bleach to psychic energies. I cleared her of these thoughts that must have caused her to obsess in seemingly self-loathing.

The Universe was showing me how effective my assistance was to her. As I left the store, I passed her while she loaded her car with groceries. Our eyes met. A subtle aspect of herself, the part of her that was aware, said thank you. She was free of a lot of the misery that showed up as negative self-talk or other people being swept into having an opinion about her.

These are the exchanges that mean something. There is no personal gain or stroking of the ego. They are the interactions that make this world a more empowering place to live. They are things that everyone is capable of doing. They are the exchanges of an awakening planet.

Addressing Mental Illness

As a medical intuitive, I can see imbalances in the body. During facilitating a recent private remote session, I could sense frays in the client's sound frequency. The impression was of skeins of yarn that were frayed from wear in a way that an overused cat scratch furniture piece would look.

To address issues at an even deeper level, one can work beyond the physicality of the client and address inconsistencies in their sound frequency or light emanation. At an understanding beyond the ego, we are an emanation of light interwoven with a frequency of sound.

While working on this one client, I could tell she was in tight control of her light emanation. It showed up as caring what people thought of her. Her sound emanation showed up frayed. This manifested as her talking too much, being singsong with her voice and conversing like everything was child's play. As I tuned in, I sensed a fray in her sound frequency.

This is something that I had never consciously pinned down before. I sensed this sort of fraying in people with bi-polar disorder that I have worked on. This woman was mentally balanced, but I still realized that perhaps I had stumbled upon a means to assist those with mental illness.

The advancements in my understanding come through my field study of private sessions. It is never just about improving the quality of life of one person. It is about tapping into the core issues that humanity deals with and addressing them by using my ability to simplify complex metaphysical dynamics and addressing the issues using the tapping, understanding and visual techniques.

Using the new understanding from my client, here are the taps that I came up with. It may be a means of correcting mental illness beyond the confines of the ego.

"I release controlling my light emanation; in all moments."

"I release controlling my sound frequency; in all moments."

"I remove murkiness from my light emanation; in all moments."

"I remove murkiness from my sound frequency; in all moments."

"I remove illusion affecting my light emanation; in all moments."

"I remove illusion affecting my sound frequency; in all moments."

"I dissipate all psychic energy affecting my light emanation; in all moments."

"I dissipate all psychic energy affecting my sound frequency; in all moments."

"I dissolve all engrams affecting my light emanation; in all moments."

"I dissolve all engrams affecting my sound frequency; in all moments."

"I remove all mental aberrations affecting my light emanation; in all moments."

"I remove all mental aberrations affecting my sound frequency; in all moments."

"I remove all schisms from my light emanation; in all moments."

"I remove all schisms from my sound frequency; in all moments."

"I untangle my light emanation; in all moments."

"I untangle my sound frequency; in all moments."

"I remove all schisms between my light emanation and my sound frequency; in all moments."

"I reintegrate my light emanation with my sound frequency; in all moments."

"I am centered and empowered in the purity of my light emanation and sound frequency; in all moments."

"I resonate, emanate and am interconnected with all life in the purity of my light emanation and sound frequency; in all moments."

THE UNIVERSAL MIND

(Say each statement three times while tapping on your head and say it a fourth time while tapping on your chest.)

"We remove all filters from the Universal mind that filter out joy; in all moments."

"We remove all filters from the Universal mind that filter out kindness; in all moments."

"We remove all filters from the Universal mind that filter out sincerity; in all moments."

"We remove all filters from the Universal mind that filter out compassion; in all moments."

"We remove all filters from the Universal mind that filter out integrity; in all moments."

"We remove all filters from the Universal mind that filter out truth; in all moments."

"We remove all filters from the Universal mind that filter out abundance; in all moments."

"We remove all filters from the Universal mind that filter out freedom; in all moments."

"We remove all filters from the Universal mind that filter out health; in all moments."

"We remove all filters from the Universal mind that filter out success; in all moments."

"We remove all filters from the Universal mind that filter out justice; in all moments."

"We remove all filters from the Universal mind that filter out accountability; in all moments."

"We remove all filters from the Universal mind that filter out equality; in all moments."

"We remove all filters from the Universal mind that filter out freedom; in all moments."

"We remove all filters from the Universal mind that filter out peace; in all moments."

"We remove all filters from the Universal mind that filter out accountability; in all moments."

"We remove all filters from the Universal mind that filter out discernment; in all moments."

"We remove all filters from the Universal mind that filter out beauty; in all moments."

"We remove all filters from the Universal mind that filter out connectedness; in all moments."

"We remove all filters from the Universal mind that filter out worthiness; in all moments."

"We remove all filters from the Universal mind that filter out enthusiasm; in all moments."

"We remove all filters from the Universal mind that filter out enlightenment; in all moments."

"We remove all filters from the Universal mind that enhance corruption; in all moments."

"We remove all filters from the Universal mind that enhance depression; in all moments."

"We remove all filters from the Universal mind that enhance greed; in all moments."

"We remove all filters from the Universal mind that propagate ignorance; in all moments."

"We remove all filters from the Universal mind that enhance isolation; in all moments."

"We remove all filters from the Universal mind that propagate hate; in all moments."

"We remove all filters from the Universal mind that propagate unworthiness; in all moments."

"We remove all filters from the Universal mind that proliferate disease; in all moments."

"We remove all filters from the Universal mind that proliferate destroying nature; in all moments."

"We remove all filters from the Universal mind that advance global warming; in all moments."

"We remove all filters from the Universal mind that propagate ethnic cleansing; in all moments."

"We remove all filters from the Universal mind that advance senseless war; in all moments."

"We remove all filters from the Universal mind that proliferate poverty; in all moments."

"We remove all filters from the Universal mind that enhance tribalism; in all moments."

"We remove all filters from the Universal mind that keep humanity trapped in primal mode; in all moments."

WHY ARE YOU HERE?

So many people are just watching the news and lamenting what a shitty place this world is. They use what little energy they have left to piss and moan about the state of affairs. Yet when anyone comes along who really has the intention of helping the uplifting of humanity, they get mercilessly attacked. Why?

People are terrified of fulfilling their soul contract. They are afraid to even fathom who they are beyond the illusion of this time and space. Do we really believe we just came here to lament over wanting more love and money most of our days? Then when all hope of fulfilling our dreams of more love and money evaporate, we turn our energy to the fear of death?

Are we still really so manipulated? Can't we see breaks in the tapestry of illusion? If God is love, why are we so trained to hate? Why do our particular beliefs forbid us from questioning? If the factions of truth are in charge, why is there so much suffering in the world? Why do the people who come here to help uplift humanity, like myself, meet so much derision?

Who are you as a spiritual being? I get attacked so many times by people who are on a supposed spiritual path and are so interested in what I share. When I say attacked, I am not talking about snide comments. I am talking about literal energetic attacks beyond this world of illusion. They want me gone. They demonize my message so that others avoid truth.

They like what I say for a while and if I say one thing that doesn't fit with their understanding, they resent me and end up attacking or avoiding me like the plague. They end up aligning with a more comfortable path where one will instill dominance and tell them what to do, all the while making them believe that they are empowering them.

They keep them trapped in a mental holding cell and removed from their purpose. They are part of the spiritual elite that believe they know what is best for everyone but want to keep the masses ignorant of truth so they can be superior.

What I do here is share truth beyond the veil of illusion. I take very complicated concepts for those entrenched in illusion and allow truth to filter back into their very conditioned physical brain. In energy, some are cowering and shackled. But the truth I share literally sets them free. I give them taps to help them find love and attract money, but I am doing more. Love and money are the dangling carrots. They will be more free to receive them. But I am using their human desire for love and money to show them how to empower themselves once again.

It has been a long time, in a reality very far away, that most of you have really felt empowered. This desire plays out in your preferences for war games and movies. It also plays out in a desire to know your purpose. At the core, you know this world is not fulfilling. The illusion provided has run its course. At one time you thought it was only you who was feeling this way. Now you are starting to understand through social media that there is a universal desperation to be empowered.

Because there are still so few of us living our soul contract, we get attacked for trying to break the programming and conditioning that occurs. You have even experienced such shifts in the algorithms of social media. The more that we share positive beneficial posts to support each other, the less our posts are shared. That is not an accident. That is by design by factions that wish to use social media to keep us divided rather than allow us to realize our empowerment.

If any of this resonates, please do the exercise of taps below. If you have been wondering what your life purpose is, please do these taps. If you worry about the suffering of others and are tired of feeling helpless, please do these taps. If you have outgrown the belief systems of group factions that seem to teach hate instead of love, please do these taps. If you have benefited from anything I have posted and it has stirred something within you about your own empowerment, please do these taps.

As more of you awaken and step up to your responsibilities as an empowered being, the easier it will get for all to be empowered. The fear will dry up and also more of the illusion. There will be more of a place for truth, love, kindness and creativity in the world as universal practices, and not just to line the pockets of the entitled.

(Say each statement three times while tapping on your head and say a fourth time while tapping on your chest.)

"I do these taps for myself and as a surrogate for all souls; in all moments."

"I make space in all worlds to activate the fulfillment of my soul's contract; in all moments."

"I remove all blockages in all worlds to the activation of the fulfillment of my soul's contract; in all moments."

"I open all portals in all worlds to the activation of the fulfillment of my soul's contract; in all moments."

"I eliminate the first cause in the deactivation of the fulfillment of my soul's contract; in all moments."

"I stretch my capacity to activate and follow through with the fulfillment of my soul's contract; in all moments."

"I am centered and empowered in the activation and fulfillment of my soul's contract; in all moments."

"I resonate, emanate and am interconnected with all life in the activation of my soul's contract; in all moments."

After you have done these taps, please leave a message that you have done them so others may gain the incentive to do them as well. So many people are looking on, yet hesitant to do the actual tapping. The tapping is a method to assist the individuals in getting past their resistance to truth. Not wanting to actually do the taps is the conditioning that needs to be penetrated. The tapping does this.

MANIFESTING PEACE

hy Try?

    The reason that it is important to keep up yourself and your home is not to compete with others. It is a means to raise your own vibration to match the vibration of which you desire to attract. If you want to be surrounded by beauty, put out the intention to make yourself beautiful.

If you want peace in the world, clean out the chaos in your own vibration so you yourself match the vibration of peace and hold space for peace. In this way, you will be like a note on a page of music that carries the song along.

By holding space for peace, you open up a corridor for peace within yourself. Allow peace to breeze through your consciousness and rush forth into humanity with a new fervor.

Prevent Civil War

There are psychic energies that are goading the dejected, unfulfilled, angry people of the world to lash out and voice their discontent and feel empowered by waging a civil war. They are fed through biased media, the outrage of an unfair society that overlooks their need to be validated.

The mouthpieces of such ignoble intentions are millionaires using the people they stir up as pawns in their power plays.

There is a spiritual awakening brewing and it can happen easily while sidestepping mass bloodshed and outrage over a political agenda. Please don't be used as a pawn.

There are ways of bowing out of this mass hypnotism. It involves catching yourself whenever you feel angry at current events and just withdrawing your energy from them. But it is hard to do from the vantage point of either side. Because you know you are right.

I, being a very dynamic Shaman, can dissipate these psychic energies that work to hypnotize and stir up people. I do my best alone, but the more people who use their love and kindness consciously, the more helpful they are in dampening the flames of a civil war.

Please know that those who are afraid to transcend drag their heels by lashing out or digging in with the most egregious power plays. They are merely afraid of the inevitable. I personally would like to see everyone awaken in a gentle way and not through the shedding of blood and more suffering. We all have enough of that stored in our Akashic records.

There is an outdated spiritual belief that the earth is a warring planet and cannot come to peace. That is a belief system perhaps of the third dimension and not the fifth. There is also the belief that there is always one more step spiritually. That would make the case that the world would eventually turn to peace as well, since peace is our natural state in the higher realms.

For anyone who hasn't participated in doing my taps yet, please know that they are a powerful way to tap into your mind potential without being limited by the will of the ego. Your mind is a 3D printer that can manifest the most incredible outcomes. The taps I share allow you to realize your potential before your belief system has evolved to support it.

You are capable of amazing feats. Please overcome your resistance. The resistance is you pulling your energy out of psychic quicksand

and enabling yourselves and others in a way that you aren't likely to believe yet.

(Say each statement three times while tapping on your head and say it a fourth time while tapping on your chest.)

"I declare myself a surrogate for humanity in doing these taps; in all moments."

"I release being used as a pawn in a power faction's agenda; in all moments."

"I release overlooking my own kindness, beauty, abilities and purpose; in all moments."

"I release being deduced to a grunt by outrage and indignation; in all moments."

"I release hating my beautiful brethren; in all moments."

"I release overlooking the kindness, beauty, abilities and purpose of my beautiful brethren; in all moments."

"I dissipate the psychic energy that is revved up by indignation; in all moments."

"I release being stoked by bias news shows; in all moments."

"I dissipate the psychic energy that is evoked by watching bias news shows and owning guns; in all moments."

"I release being locked in primal mode; in all moments."

"I remove all engrams of the civil war; in all moments."

"I dissipate all the psychic energy of the primal mode; in all moments."

"I free all souls trapped in the hell of the civil war; in all moments."

"I release romanticizing the civil war; in all moments."

"I dissipate the psychic energy of the civil war; in all moments."

"I send all energy matrices into the light and sound that advocate war; in all moments."

"All complex energy matrices that advocate war are escorted into the light and sound; in all moments."

"I send all energy matrices into the light and sound that wield power over others; in all moments."

"All complex energy matrices that wield power over others are escorted into the light and sound; in all moments."

"I send all energy matrices into the light and sound that manipulate the masses; in all moments."

"All complex energy matrices that manipulate the masses are escorted into the light and sound; in all moments."

"I dissipate all causal energy of the civil war; in all moments."

"I release carrying a grudge from one life to the next; in all moments."

"I eliminate the first cause in the starting of civil war; in all moments."

"I release being coerced, manipulated, brainwashed or seduced into civil war; in all moments."

"I relinquish the hate; in all moments."

"I convert all hate into kindness; in all moments."

"I radically accept self-love; in all moments."

"I release taking personally the dismantling of power factions; in all moments."

"I close all portals to civil war; in all moments."

"I dissipate the psychic energy of self-righteousness and convert it into kindness; in all moments."

"I strip all illusion off of the power factions; in all moments."

"I shift my paradigm from primal mode to enlightenment; in all moments."

"I recant all vows and agreements between myself and civil; war; in all moments."

"I recant all vows and agreements to all power factions; in all moments."

"I withdraw all my energy from the civil war; in all moments."

"I withdraw all my energy from all power factions; in all moments."

"I easily awaken; in all moments."

"I shift my paradigm from war to peace; in all moments."

"I shift the world from war to peace; in all moments."

"I am centered and empowered in peace; in all moments."

"The world is centered and empowered in peace; in all moments."

"I resonate, emanate and am interconnected with all life in peace; in all moments."
"The world resonates, emanates, and is interconnected with all life in peace; in all moments."

A Dog's Karma

Buster rolled down the back window and jumped out. I didn't realize it. I looked in the back seat and he was gone!! I was terrified. I was a whole town away before I discovered it. Bernie was trying to tell me.

I got back into the car and drove frantically to the street where I saw the window roll down. It felt like forever. I was doing all kinds of energy work. If I can do it for others, I can do it for my own babies.

Sure enough, as I turned down the street, there was Buster waiting at the curb for me with a nice man petting him. I screamed, "Buster!" The man had called Animal Control and was waiting for it. He mentioned that a couple of times, like he wanted me to wait and be held accountable. Buster had no tags.

I had explained that Buster was chipped, but it caused irritation in him and that it was removed. Also, every time I had put tags on him, Bernie would get them off him during rough play. They had even eaten two expensive flea collars. One collar they ate twice. Buster threw it up and they ate it again. I have tried to keep tags on them both.

Buster would have no part of the lecture on the way home. He was avoiding the stinging words at all cost. They weren't harsh words. I was just trying to get a little accountability from him. He would have none of it.

I was contemplating why this event had happened. I was talking to Buster and telling him how worried I was, and I rushed right back to get him as soon as I knew he was gone. I told him over and over how worried I was and how sad I was without him with me. These words soothed his soul.

Then I remembered how I knew that Buster was my dog in a past life of his. I had given him up for some reason. I had abandoned him. As a puppy I knew he worried that I would abandon him again. It was the core issue of all his fights with his littermate Bernie. Abandonment is a painful core issue.

As I was telling Buster how worried I was when he was gone and how I was frantically driving to get back to him, I could sense his deep satisfaction. It was more than just a smile on his big happy mug. It was the core issue that he had brought into this life being evaporated away.

He was so worried that I would abandon him. The scab of that core issue was ripped raw today when I inadvertently drove off without him. His pain was exposed in real time. But then I returned. I showed real remorse of missing him. I poured my relief into him. That core issue of abandonment can now heal in him. My wonderful, sweet boy now realizes how much he is loved and how important he is to me. No worries. Mamma will come find you.

Today, Buster worked through his karma of abandonment. It was merely an emotional wound that he was unable to process at the time. So it is with so many karmic imbalances. As with Buster, so it is with us all. This is the lifetime to heal. This is the lifetime to be validated. This is the lifetime to heal others. This is the lifetime to validate others.

Vantage Point

The Zen of life is that those with purpose use their passion and talents to touch as many people as possible. At the same time, they are deflecting from an onslaught of attacks in their personal realm. It is like the process of transcending is about expanding yourself while a million arrows are trying to make a direct hit to ground you.

This is the formula experience. The truth is that no one can take you down. No assault, rejection, abandonment, humiliation or dead-on hit can keep you down. The only thing that can defeat you is you. If you turn your attention from that of your passion to the assault at hand, you invert your own intention.

Once you see yourself as the victim, then the negative energies pestering you will be effective. You are no victim. You are being targeted because your energy is too positive for mainstream. Negativity collects on it as readily as water condenses on a cold glass on a hot day. It is not personal.

Once you make it personal, the plight of yourself as a victim takes on new life. It is up to you to stay in your passion and what you love with such incredible love for those receiving. This affords you the most expansive vantage point to deter you from losing hope or introvert in any way.

Love humanity. Love it for all it is capable of being. Have compassion and kindness for everyone who is still fighting with their own ego. Of course, they will project anything they can onto you if possible. They can't handle the disappointment that they are living with.

Love them beyond their own disappointment. Continue to see their potential. Speak to them through their higher angels. Your ability to see them empowered may be the bootstrap they need to pull themselves up with. Being able to hold space for their higher angels may be your greatest gift to humanity in manifestation.

This is raising your vantage point to the Highest Love.

THE ENERGETIC PROTEST

The nuclear backfire that happened in the world was possibly a consequence of the taps we do. The amazing, brave protests we are seeing around the world where people are dying for their personal freedoms is a result of our taps.

It is unfortunate that when people in other countries are risking their lives for freedom, we here are so complacent as our democracy is being taken from us. We piss it away by getting distracted by hype, fighting about peripheral issues and demonizing those who present us with the truth. All the while, the president sends his son over to make a land deal with China.

The Squad is not the enemy. Immigrants are not the enemy. Pro-choice laws are not the enemy. The enemy is those who sit in office and do nothing as a traitor runs our decency and values down to the ground to make more dollars in his pocket. Daddy can't bank roll him, so he gets bankrolled by the most ruthless monsters that have ever put on a human garb.

If you don't want to protest, stop the enabling of the monsters who don't care if children suffer needlessly. The monsters who have no compassion and no qualms about creating suffering to make a few bucks. Try doing the taps. It's a version of protest that is effective under the surface.

Try these:

(Say each statement three times while tapping on your head and say it a fourth time while tapping on your chest.)

"We release enabling the monsters; in all moments."

"We reveal the monsters in their true form; in all moments."

"We release the cowering in indifference; in all moments."

"We immediately thwart the attacking of innocence; in all moments."

"We wake everyone up from the sleep of apathy; in all moments."

"We break truth through the cracks to create a barrage of understanding; in all moments."

"We dismantle all state-owned media; in all moments."

"We expose all the monsters and ruthlessly hold them accountable; in all moments."

"We dissipate the psychic distraction of infighting; in all moments."

"We refuse to be deterred by distractions; in all moments."

"We save democracy; in all moments."

"We shift the world's paradigm from money controlled to democracy; in all moments."

"We protect, inspire and empower all avatars of truth; in all moments."

"We hold space for a world-wide synergy between all avatars of truth; in all moments."

"We make space in the world for universal peace, empowerment and freedom; in all moments."

"We remove all blockages to universal peace, empowerment and freedom; in all moments."

"We stretch our capacity to manifest and maintain universal peace, empowerment and freedom; in all moments."

"We are centered and empowered in universal peace, empowerment and freedom; in all moments."

"We resonate, emanate and are interconnected with all life in universal peace, empowerment and freedom; in all moments."

Please know that even one person doing these taps can create great change in the world. Just like one Gandhi or Mother Theresa afforded the world with great change as well.

THIS I IMPLORE

Please write or message Pope Francis and ask him to unseal the secret writings that talk about reincarnation. The ones that were omitted from the Bible by those who wanted to charge for passage to heaven during corrupt eras.

If Pope Francis would reveal those writings, then the mystery of when life begins would be clearer. Just as it is written in Genesis that God made the body of Adam and then breathed life into it, it will be understood that life begins at the first breath.

Also, there is a spiritual law that no two souls can operate the same space at the same time. It is not possible for there to be a soul contained within the soul of another person. This is as ridiculous as it comes.

Please write or message Pope Francis to reveal all of the references to reincarnation that were taken out of the version of the Bible that we are privy to. The one life scenario began in the Dark Ages and the Dark Ages is where we continue to land until all souls realize the depth of their lifespan.

Everyone we love and everything we fear has been determined by past life experiences. Society is collected in a shallow pool of ignorance with the limited self-awareness they are able to glean in a one life scenario.

Living your life as if it began and ends with this lifetime is as limiting as stepping into the middle of a classic novel and believing you can understand the depth of the main character by one thin chapter.

The reason there is so much judgment and corruption in the world is because individuals have stepped away from the spiritual journey of self-discovery. They have landed believing all their traits and merits were born and raised within this one lifetime. We are so much more multidimensional than this. Innately we know this, and it causes us to lash out in frustration.

The reason so many people are interested in researching their ancestors is that they are looking for themselves in a peripheral way that is socially acceptable. The truth is that the adventures and tribu-lations that we have endured play out in our dreams and manifest in our interactions and life choices.

Let's stop distracting ourselves in the petty pursuit of a purist state. We have all played the role of the whore, the beast, the temptress, the warlord and the slave master. It is more productive to stop judging others by an unnatural morality that is only maintained under the highest scrutiny of control. It is much more productive to embrace the organic essence of our own flaws.

These flaws are the seedbed of our compassion and tolerance in dealing with others. If we can see something in others that causes a reaction, it is us reacting to our own unresolved issues. It is much more productive to the evolution of humanity if we turn our scope inward and reveal the depth of our own pain.

Rip off the scabs and pull back the floorboards on our own denial. When we can look in the mirror and see the flawed, broken, corrupted, defeated and terrified creature looking back at us and we can afford it some love and kindness, then the corruption and the systemic bullying in the world will recede and all individuals can awaken and repair their deepest schisms.

Please ask Pope Francis to fulfill his true purpose. The lineage of corrupt men held the title of Pope so this one pure soul could hold space now to resurrect truth. His purpose is as humble and dynamic as many others who have returned to earth at this time. He is here to reveal the truth of reincarnation to the masses. This will fulfill his true destiny among men.

This will end the violation into a woman's body functions to demean and demoralize her. Gaia is ready to reclaim her place in empowerment. We as individuals are here to assist. As we reclaim our own Gaia energy; including kindness, compassion and the ability to discern, all individuals will awaken and the path to World Peace will ensue.

ASSISTING MASS AWAKENING

❦

tepping Up the Pace of Awakening
 Awakening isn't something that happens "out there." Awakening is the process of every individual reclaiming their empowerment in both subtle and demonstrative ways.

The demonstrative ways have to do with speaking up when there is a lower narrative being highlighted, using your gifts to forgo the linear enslavement of conformity that happens through seeking security, and through raising the vibration of every moment possible through kindness.

The subtle ways of assisting awakening is addressing the internal thought streams that are bombarding your psyche continuously. People think that their thoughts are their own. When the truth is, they are immersed in, and bombarded by, a river of thoughts at any one moment.

The thoughts that you choose to claim are the ones that you give life to, merely by acknowledging them. The ones you choose may depend on your level of awareness. Those who are aware of the dynamics of this thought stream that we are immersed in may choose very carefully to give life to positive thoughts.

Yet, it can be a constant struggle to pick worthy thoughts to enliven and give intention to, unless one realizes the dynamics that are in play. If one is not aware of the bombardment of thoughts, they will be at the mercy of the most negative feelings and thoughts. Because just as there are thought streams that one is immersed in, there are also psychic streams of energy that bombard the individual to affect their emotional state as well.

Being one that chooses positive thoughts and emotions is a way to affect the consciousness of the collective. Yet the more one chooses neutrality in their thoughts and feelings, the more it purifies the airwaves that we are all immersed in.

For example, those feelings of regret that you have been having, the ones that ruthlessly remind you of past failings or mistakes, are bombarding the masses right now. Many people are going through the same feelings of lamenting the choices of the past. This is a means to prevent the masses from awakening.

Lamenting the past or thinking about the past in a longing way is a means to prevent humanity from awakening. Thinking about the past is a way to give it teeth to stay gripped to the present. Awakening is a means of sloughing off old consciousness and beginning anew at such a higher vibratory rate. Being emotionally attached to the past is a means to give it life and to bog down the birth of new consciousness by obsessing over the past.

Staying present with your thoughts in the present is a great way to assist the collective to awaken. Every time a thought or feeling comes through, use your abilities of discernment to realize its randomness and forgo giving it life through your attention. This may seem very difficult at first because the thoughts and feelings slip in and seem so personal. But the more you choose positive or neutral thoughts and feelings, the more freedom you will experience.

What you will be doing in energy is creating space in these streams of thought and psychic energy for others to be less bombarded by them. You will be lessening their grip on others just as the truth lessens the effectiveness of a lie.

So, the technique to use is this: Every time you find yourself thinking about the past, consciously bring yourself to the present and express some gratitude for your present-day situation. If you find yourself going into the past, realize that you are not alone and pull yourself back to the present. In doing so, you will empower others to pull themselves back to the present as well.

A lot of depression, and self-regret can dry up as a result of your efforts. Think of regret as the doorway to hell and gratitude the gateway to heaven. Every time you take a moment to self-reflect, ask yourself if you are indulging in heaven or hell. The choices that you choose will eventually become easier.

THE MISGUIDANCE of Asking for Prayers

Whenever there is a tragedy, people are so quick to ask for prayers from anyone. That is a misguided understanding of the dynamics of energy and what is really occurring.

Many times, the people that are the subject of prayer requests are already jammed up with stagnant energy that they did not know how to release. That is why it is stagnant. Energy should move freely throughout the body. Like a river always flowing through and emptying out and being replenished. Or better yet, energy should always emanate out in all directions like a sunburst.

When energy is not moving this readily, there is a blockage formed somewhere. It can be an emotional issue, a belief collected along the way or a past experience that was so traumatic that it made its way to the surface tension of the energy field of the person. It manifests as a discomfort or dis-ease.

When one is dealing with these energy blockages, the last thing they need is more energy added to the issue to dam it up even worse. Not to mention that there are peripheral issues that come with the prayers that are sent. Limiting thoughts, emotional projections and past experiences of the sender of the prayers can be added to the mix.

In a way, asking for prayers for someone is a violation to their personal rights. I always get annoyed when people take images of others in the hospital as well. Is this the image of themselves that people want to be known and remembered as? Perpetually in a hospital bed with hoses up their nose?

It is a violation to another to portray them this way. Even if both are ignorant of what they are doing. The person who is taking the picture is shoving this imagery of another into the psyche of others' minds, which are 3D printers, even if they don't realize their magnitude. It is hard to recover from mass sympathy induced by seeing a loved one in their most vulnerable state.

The person who is asking for prayers is most likely having trouble coping with the fact that they feel helpless. They are giving their power away even more, instead of realizing that it only takes one dynamic intention to assist someone in getting over their issues. It doesn't usually consist of adding energy through prayers. It actually consists of extracting all the stagnant energy in the body and encouraging the person's own energy system to continue to function and to flow.

As for taking pictures of someone in a hospital, the one sharing is doing a disservice to the subject involved. They are getting people who don't even know the person to agree, in some subtle way, that this image is the best that person can do; that this is their normal. It does not mean that to the person who loves them because of the love factor. But you can't get people to love those they see in a distressed position. Maybe when we all awaken, but not yet.

The other dynamic thing that happens when someone is asked to send prayers is that you can't vet the people who will send them. There are some people who are great at sending energy, but the quality of energy is tainted by their own issues unless they really understand the dynamics of what they are doing.

If someone is trying to heal, it is an extra burden to send them energy that is filled with the needs, wants, insecurities and other lacks that the sender may inadvertently add to the prayers. To think that all energy sent is pure is naive at best, and dangerous at worst.

It makes a great social media post to ask for prayers. But mostly people who ask for prayers are asking for love for themselves. Which is fine and honest but can be done without involving a person who really needs to be left to heal.

Why not assume that all people could use some love and validation and send it out to all others in all ways. That way, we will be training ourselves to emanate out in all directions and will get out of targeting anyone in the linear sense of sick, feeble or hopeless.

THE DREAM VALIDATION

I have known for some time now that all group dynamics are toxic for the individual's growth. Recently, I had a dream experience that explained why. It played out the dynamic of groups.

I was in a home with all my pets (they represented all those whom I feel comfortable with) and there was also a beautiful woman from one of the television shows I used to watch who played a savvy lawyer, and a man I was familiar with.

The dream took place in an apartment that apparently in the dream was my comfort zone. The woman and the man were there in my comfort zone. The woman was sitting on the couch next to me and we were interacting. But then the man came over to give us a group hug (creating a group consciousness). All the time he was hugging me, I couldn't speak; I couldn't move; I could hardly breathe. But he didn't notice.

He was impervious to me. He was more focused on the beautiful woman. This symbolized how groups are focused on the most superficial issues and impervious to what goes on with the individual or under the surface. I explained how uncomfortable the hug was, but he didn't listen. He leaned in for two more hugs at different times.

This represented how group dynamics (represented by the hug) were all still initiated by male energy (the woman and I were content to sit next to each other on the couch) and it was the male energy that was getting its needs met through the interaction. Male energy is empowered by group settings.

For female energy, the group dynamic isn't necessary. Because female energy can glean all she needs to from subtle perceptions and agreements. It was male energy that needed it all spelled out specifically in the group dynamics.

Later in the dream, the male energy and I were spooning in an intimate setting. He was lying behind me as we both rested (it symbolized coexisting equally). Then, I felt him try to penetrate me from behind. It was so weak and ineffective that I wasn't sure. It was very ineffective at being anything pleasant.

I got up and went in the kitchen still unsure if we had an actual encounter. He came out with such bravado and self-fulfillment that I got my answer that we had a sexual encounter. He was then very demonstrative with me and was acting like we were now in a relationship. I just watched myself go along with it. This was playing out the subtle way female energy gets overtaken by male energy and just goes along with it.

The meaning was that all group settings are based on fulfilling superficial needs. The male energy will dominate because it is male energy's nature to thrive in group settings which are not necessary for female energy.

In the group setting, female energy and the empowerment of the individual is paralyzed. Female energy is comfortable as individuals, but male energy is more apt to form the group setting. And even when the female energy thinks that it has come to terms with male energy, male energy will always try its best to dominate female energy and operate as if it has dominion.

Female energy must always hold its stance and never again be complacent with male energy. Male energy has nearly run this world to the ground. It is female energy that must save it by holding her stance of empowerment.

It is female energy that has compassion and understanding of others. That must be her focus. Because if she allows male energy to override her through complacency, the subtle senses are lost to his superficial understanding of dynamics. We are seeing this played out in the world.

. . .

BE *a Portal for Truth*

(Say each statement three times while tapping on your head and say it a fourth time while tapping on your chest.)

"We make space in this world for truth to surface; in all moments."

"We dissipate all the psychic energy that thwarts the surfacing of truth; in all moments."

"We open all portals to the surfacing of truth; in all moments."

"We remove all blockages to the surfacing of truth; in all moments."

"We send all energy matrices into the light and sound that thwart the surfacing of truth; in all moments."

"We command all complex energy matrices that thwart truth to be escorted into the light and sound; in all moments."

"We stretch the capacity of humanity to recognize and accept truth; in all moments."

"Humanity is centered and empowered in recognizing and accepting truth; in all moments."

"Humanity emanates, resonates and is interconnected with all life in recognizing and accepting truth; in all moments."

THE PICTURES *in Your Mind*

The pictures in your mind are old engrams of past failures breaking up and releasing from your construct. But you recognize them and identify with them and so pull them back to you and linoleum your life with them.

This is also happening in the macrocosm. That is why issues we thought we had surpassed are coming back to the surface to address, such as bigotry, judgment, the abortion issue, the measles outbreak and others.

They are not returning because we are supposed to relive them. These are things that we have surpassed and learned from. But many terrified souls are trying to enliven them because as dark and ominous as our past is, some people are more terrified of their own accountability and even empowerment.

It is now time for all individuals to withdraw their clutch on a group mentality--The Primal Fear of Being. Separation from the herd must be confronted so that each individual can feel the surge and thrust of their own empowerment.

It is not done by demeaning and taking from others but by separating who you are as an exponential being from a linear and limiting timeline. We are all empowered in the collective and the irony is that the way to embrace this strength is to separate from the group mentality and embrace our individuality. Get this!

THE COLLECTIVE

It is wonderful to be invited into a celebration when people share their happy events. This is how social media should be used. It adds to the collective instead of weighing it down with personal tragedies. When will humans understand?

There are healing factions working relentlessly to pull people out of their funk. They are working so hard to try and wrestle people's issues away from them. Most people don't need mass prayers to heal their issues. At this point, all they need is to step away from them for a short bit so the Universe can recalibrate.

The ego is so desperate to not give up claims, that it works overtime to hang onto any issue that would be naturally cleansed away. We are seeing this on a mass scale through social issues. Don't take the bait.

Use your higher understanding to stay separated from social issues that are rearing up again. Address them. But address them without being sucked into the psychic energy of 'them versus us,' or the cyclical patterns of self-righteousness.

The self-righteousness that the awakened may feel is of the same vibration of self-righteousness that may embolden the susceptible to judge and wield self-righteousness for ill-gotten gains of power and corruption.

The better strategy is compassion and kindness for those still under the influence of psychic control. Compassion and kindness dry up psychic influence if administered with awareness. Jumping into the emotional fray merely feeds the issues one and all of the awakened strive to dissipate.

THE CURE

The core issue is when you were in agreement with power. It is too unbearable to think that in our past lives we were amongst the power mongers who take so readily from humanity. Looking at the world around us, we are devastated with the corruption.

We would be crushed to realize that our choices, alliances and agreements in past eras led to the current state of worldly affairs. People need to believe that they are good. That is why they cling to the one life scenario, so they can rest in the denial that they came into the world innocent and pure.

But our DNA carries the memory card of all our past lives. This is the correlation between disease and our DNA. Our DNA and the diseases that it reveals is a coping mechanism for the aspects of ourselves that we refuse to accept in our waking physical state.

If we believe on the surface that we are innocent, how does the whole self or innate wisdom rectify the transgressions that the whole self is aware of? Perhaps genetic diseases are self-inflicted punishment for transactions the surface self is oblivious to.

The cure to this dynamic is to embrace the depth of one's self and to understand that everyone is multidimensional in the fact we have all been the tyrant and the oppressors. Then instead of running to church to reinforce the denial that we are good, we can relax in our atoms and deal with the specific issues that need addressing.

Because everything we see happening in the world is a reflection of what is happening within ourselves, if we want to address world affairs, we can address them by embracing the depth of who we are.

That is why the Energetic Cleanse that I share is so powerful. It is a way to dry up the power issues within us as a means to dry up the power factions in the world. Anyone who is concerned with current events can address the angst they create by doing the

Energetic Cleanse with the most troubling issues they see in the world.

How to Dry Up Psychic Energy

There is a residual energy that is created through thoughts and feelings. It is a somewhat murky energy that collects around living beings. Some people get pretty slimy. At a certain point, this energy starts to identify with the person it is around or with others that it is subjected to. It starts to react as if they were the same; the way jello will react if its container is moved.

This personification of energy is what people have been taught to believe as entities or even evil spirits. The thing about this energy is that it grows by having a strong reaction to it. Being afraid of it feeds it. So does adding thought energy to it by thinking of it. Obsessing over it is the best thing you can do to intensify the experience of it.

The best thing you can do if something is causing you distress is to withdraw all your attention from it. Humans still don't realize what a driving force their own intentions are, especially if they are driven by fear. Harnessing people's fear is the way the power factions stay in control. It has become such a parlor trick at this point that, to some of us, it is absurd that people still fall for it.

These psychic energies can be addressed by anyone who practices the art of operating in a pure state of concentrated love. Concentrated love is not a peppy over-the-top state. That kind of love is channeled through the hormonal system and is like a sugar rush. Concentrated love is a still calmness that the individual exudes. It can be intimidating. It is as intimidating as stark truth.

Some people experience this when they encounter someone who makes them feel uncomfortable in their skin just by their presence. The reason that they are feeling uncomfortable is that some of the psychic energies that collect on someone and fortify their ego are being stripped away through the mere presence of love and truth in the intimidating person's countenance.

One can develop this cleansing agent of psychic energy through personal discipline. It involves learning NOT to react under any situation. Reactions are the way psychic energy is created. So, by forgoing reacting, one is able to stay more present to the reality at hand instead of being swept into psychic manipulation.

Non-reaction happens when one can refrain from judging anything that they are introduced to. Refrain from fear, hate and outrage. Try not to snap in a reactionary mode of taking action either. This prevents you from separating yourself from the psychic energies at hand.

Even if you are not being outwardly swayed in the moment, by kneejerk reacting you are immersing yourself in the psychic energies and making it more difficult to get free from them. I know people who have galvanized themselves in theses energies. It is more difficult to free yourselves of these energies when you think they are an aspect of you.

That is why getting your feelings hurt is not really a bad thing. If you have any intentions to be an awakened spiritual being, you will get your feelings hurt all the time. You will even feel targeted because to be crushed and to feel lost and demoralized seem to be your mainstay. This is the Universe intentionally lobbing these psychic energies off of you.

Having your feelings hurt is always a good thing in spiritual terms. The feeling bad is the raw skin of the real you being exposed. It is no different than when a crusty scab falls off and the new skin underneath feels vulnerable. When you are around someone who is awakened, these crusty energy scabs are going to be ripped off. It doesn't feel good unless the person can identify with their empowered-self and embrace the process.

The ability to dissipate the psychic energies can be developed through practice. It is done by holding a stance of a loving state unencumbered by thoughts or feelings. Society will try to motivate you into reaction by showing you an appalling image and daring you not to react.

This happens a lot with social media through showing abused animals, despicable crimes or hated political figures. The reader does not realize that they are being goaded into reacting as fuel for the very causes they detest the most. By not reacting and staying in a place of concentrated love, you do more for abused animals everywhere than sharing the image in outrage.

Sure, you can act to affect change. Just act, not react. When you act because you were introduced to some stimuli, you are being a pawn for the intention of another. If you stay in a stance of non-reaction and concentrated love, then you know that every time you act, it is to empower others, not to enslave them.

I was walking in the grocery store and came next to a very tall woman who didn't strike me as attractive. I didn't have an opinion, but as I got around her, I could hear all the insults people had encapsulated her in with their thoughts. I heard them all. If I were less aware, I would have thought they were my own thoughts. But they weren't. They were the buildup of other people's judgments that had built up on her.

It was my automatic response to strip away this ugly psychic energy that she was walking around with. It is quite easy for me to do. I simply introduce my loving intention for them to be free of the energy into manifestation. My love is like caustic bleach to psychic energies. I cleared her of these thoughts that must have caused her to obsess in seemingly self-loathing.

The Universe was showing me how effective my assistance was to her. As I left the store, I passed her while she loaded her car with groceries. Our eyes met. A subtle aspect of herself, the part of her that was aware, said thank you. She was free of a lot of the misery that showed up as negative self-talk or other people being swept into having an opinion about her.

These are the exchanges that mean something. There is no personal gain or stroking of the ego. They are the interactions that make this world a more empowering place to live. They are things that everyone is capable of doing. They are the exchanges of an awakening planet.

. . .

*THE COLLECTIVE **We***

When I start taps with 'We,' it means that when you do them, you are doing them in synergy with myself and others who do them, to make them more impactful.

(Say each statement three times while tapping on your head and say it a fourth time while tapping on your chest.)

"We dissipate the psychic energy of enabling abuse; in all moments."

"We dissipate the psychic energy that protects the abuser; in all moments."

"We dissipate the psychic energy of shaming the victim; in all moments."

"We extract all shame, guilt and doubt from the victims; in all moments."

"We strip the facade of righteousness off of all abusers; in all moments."

"We thwart the normalization of abuse; in all moments."

"We give back to all those who have been raped, shamed, humiliated, abused and broken all that has been taken from them; in all moments."

"We make whole and heal every single being that has been abused or violated; in all moments."

"We strip from all abusers all that they have taken from others and convert it back to love, healing and wholeness to those it was taken from; in all moments."

"We break all cycles of abuse; in all moments."

"We return sacred reverence to every vessel of Gaia; in all moments."

"All individuals are reconnected to their own sacred connection to Source; in all moments."

*THE BENEFITS **of Being an Individual***

The issue isn't that we aren't powerful. The issue is that we don't understand the incredible potential energy that we have when we connect the wires between our heart and mind. Why do you think so many of us have gotten beaten down to such an extent? It is because when enough of us figure out the blueprint, we will all be as effective as Gandhi, be as insightful as Einstein, be as loving as Mother Teresa and be as motivating as Mandela.

We, as individuals, are all world changers. We are made to be that. But when we throw our energy into a group and allow that group to manage our sails, we lose the breeze. We are only as great as the greatest member of our group and we are hindered by the least of them. Why not decide that humanity itself is the only thing we give our lifeblood to. We can support all the groups we want but from the vantage point of our own individuality. It is not about dropping out; it is about plugging in more.

This means thinking for ourselves, seeing the hidden agenda in every statement, feeling the energy pull of every intention and giving only to those intentions that truly benefit humanity. Once we pull ourselves free of the fibers of others' agendas, it is clearer to see the subtle form of control which we have given our power to. We can break the spell. That is the importance of claiming one's individuality.

(Say each statement three times out loud while tapping on your head and say it a fourth time while tapping on your chest.)

"I release the primal fear of being separated from the herd; in all moments."

"I release hiding in groups for security; in all moments."

"I release being enslaved to group dynamics; in all moments."

"I release being dependent on groups; in all moments."

"I release losing my identity in groups; in all moments."

"I shatter the glass ceiling of all groups; in all moments."

"I recant all vows and agreements between myself and all groups; in all moments."

"I remove all curses between myself and all groups; in all moments."

"I dissolve all karmic ties between myself and all groups; in all moments."

"I sever all strings and cords between myself and all groups; in all moments."

"I remove all the pain, burden, limitations and engrams that all groups have put on me; in all moments."

"I remove all the pain, burden, limitations and engrams that I have put on all others for the sake of a group; in all moments."

"I take back all the Joy, Love, Abundance, Freedom, Health, Success, Security, Companionship, Creativity, Peace, Life, Wholeness, Beauty, Enthusiasm, Contentment, Spirituality, Enlightenment, and Confidence that all groups have taken from me; in all moments."

"I withdraw all my energy from all groups; in all moments."

"I release resonating with all groups; in all moments."

"I release emanating with all groups; in all moments."

"I remove all groups from my sound frequency; in all moments."

"I remove all groups from my light body; in all moments."

"I shift my paradigm from all groups to Joy, Love, Abundance, Freedom, Health, Success, Security, Companionship, Creativity, Peace, Life, Wholeness, Beauty, Enthusiasm, Contentment, Spirituality, Enlightenment and Confidence; in all moments."

"I transcend all groups; in all moments."

"I am centered and empowered in the divinity of my own individuality; in all moments."

"I make space in this world for the realization of the empowerment of my own individuality; in all moments."

"I remove all blockages to the realization of the empowerment of my own individuality; in all moments."

"I stretch my capacity to manifest and accept the empowerment of my own individuality; in all moments."

"I am centered and empowered in Divine Love; in all moments."

Think about it, have you ever really been honored to your full potential in any group? Have you ever soared to your greatest heights? Have the groups on earth honored all its members? Have they disparaged non-members? The only group that is going to honor all life is the one where all are included equally. That is the group of humanity, where all are important.

. . .

THINKING *from the Whole*

The way anything is expanded or anything moves in energy, is from the highest intention. If you were to see yourself as a magnificent galaxy, it would be easier to clear out the stagnant energy of greed and corruption on one little planet like Earth.

The trouble is that humans have been ensconced in the human condition and have lost a lot of ability to stretch their imagination. The imagination is a powerful force in expanding consciousness. Every advantage to humanity has been afforded through the imagination.

Those who are considered flaky, delusional, or on the fringe of society, are the ones who regularly tap into the fruits of the imagination. They are demonized for it. But look around. If the imagination is such a bad thing, why is this world that lacks imagination doing so poorly? Why do we flock to the concerts and art openings of the creative people with imagination? Why can we not expand the creative imagination within ourselves?

Every person who is different, unique, or sees the world in a different way is feeling the call of their own creativity. The more imaginative energy that individuals release, that is not harnessed for the advancement of big business, the more the world can be expanded to hold space for world peace.

PLEASE STOP SENDING *Prayers*

When I am feeling what others call sick, it is because there is too much turbulence in my energy field. I don't think of myself as a body but more like a solar system of energy. This expansiveness allows for more dynamic effects in assisting others.

Since they are most likely identifying with the microcosm of them, I, being in galaxy mode, can just acknowledge them and bring an issue to a calm. But anyone could do this if they had my experience and determination. But they have their own and will do what they do in their own way.

When people send me prayers, they are generally sending thought aberrations. I feel their limitations in understanding and all the hopelessness that initiated their desperate adherence to prayer. The thought forms are coarse and limiting.

When people send me energy, it creates nausea in me. I am working hard at that point to maintain a calm. Their energy comes through and churns the water around me. It makes it harder to return to a calm. When people send love, they are really sending thought forms. Because we are immersed in love, what is needed is to release all the coarse vibrations intruding on that reality.

If people want to help me, they will send love to the whole world. The reason I get taxed is because I am working to dissipate the psychic energies that have engulfed the earth. Pure love and intentions without judgment can dissipate the psychic energies, but people are untrained in doing that. They are more conditioned to curse all of humanity by stating how nasty people are or how screwed up the planet is.

You can't be effective as a healer with this shroud of opinions laying over you. You have to be able to see with your spiritual eyes the perfection of your subject and use your convictions to manifest that pristine version of them.

Many people walk on tip toes around me. They say they are afraid of doing the wrong thing. But I interact with everyone that comes to me from the state of our equal perfection. The joy, love, abundance, freedom and health are our natural state. The things that they really are afraid of is all the stuff that interferes with them perceiving themselves in that perfect state.

By the way, just seeing others as that dynamo is the healing process. It is that simple. But that is not in general what is done. People will fixate on the flaws or the issues; they will give sympathy to raise their own vantage point in comparison, and they will even curse others by attaching labels to them.

Every label you put on someone is a curse. At birth we label a child by their genitals. They are either boy or girl, but so many people are cursed by that one innocent well-intentioned label. Saying one is a boy precludes him from his feelings and sweetness. Saying one is a girl curses her to life of subtle discrimination. See?

A great form of healing is to refuse to put any labels on anyone. It's not better if it is complimentary. Do you know how hard it is to suffer under the yoke of being the nice one? Being good at all costs comes with the disadvantage of innate limitations.

If you really want to help someone heal, see them as whole and empowered. Hold space for that. Don't over emphasize this in words though, because it can come across as invalidation of the person's plight. Giving them sympathy can be immersing them in emotional quicksand.

If someone has issues, see them or anyone as healthy and in their prime. Don't send prayers or energy. If they are sensitive, these could be making them nauseous. It is better to release all that needs to be released from yourself so that you are clear and just be present with them energetically.

Energy systems share information. The stronger energy system will correct the interrupted one. That is why animals are so healing. Their unencumbered energy system will repair yours that is riddled with hindering thoughts and limitations. The love is pure and is not waiting to have its ego stroked too much.

If you want to heal others, just think of all their good qualities until it opens you and them up in gratitude. This is healing. If you do this in energy, the person will feel it. If you value how well that works, visualize yourself magnified or multiplied a billion times over and hold space with all those who are suffering in the world. Do this from a place beyond reproach.

It is the healing thing to do.

FINISHING PROJECTS

So many people struggle with finishing projects. If this is an issue for you, here are some core issues to do the Energetic Cleanse in Chapter 13.

Insert each of these phrases one at a time into all the sentences and do the taps with them:

- Lifetimes of failure
- Confusing my purpose with lifetimes of failure
- Dying too soon
- Confusing completing projects with the unattainable
- Confusing restarting a project with a new incarnation

PROTECT *the Rain Forests*

I have been posting taps and visualizations for years. It has only been in the last couple of years that people have recognized the powerful healing results in doing the taps. Some may look at the world and see it worse than ever. But the fact that so many people are paying attention is an upgrade in humanity.

If people had done the taps I share in social media years ago, maybe it would have prevented so many alarming current events. Perhaps we need to be pushed up against our issues to act.

If you have never tried my taps, maybe this is your call to try them. The rainforests belong to the earth. They are a part of all of us. If you are alarmed with them burning, then please try these taps:

(Say each statement three times while tapping on your head and say it a fourth time while tapping on your chest.)

(I phrase the statements using 'We' because all who are reading and doing the taps create a synergy of Einstein's doing the taps together.)

"We immediately extinguish all the fires in the rain forest: in all moments."

"We immediately oust all those who desecrate the rain forests; in all moments."

"We slap the wrists of all those who sell out the rain forests; in all moments."

"We activate a shroud of protection around the rainforests and all sacred lands; in all moments."

"We regenerate the rain forests; in all moments."

"We hold the rainforests in a sovereign state of grace; in all moments."

"We make space in this world for the rainforests to regenerate and thrive; in all moments."

"We remove all blockages to the rainforests regenerating and thriving; in all moments."

"We stretch our capacity to protect the regeneration of the rainforests; in all moments."

"We are centered and empowered in the protection and regeneration of the rainforests; in all moments."

"We resonate, emanate and are interconnected with all life in the protection and regeneration of the rainforests; in all moments."

POSITIVE TAPS *Do the following sets of taps with The Positive Protocol (below)*

- Fulfilling my purpose in one lifetime
- Complete my projects
- Fulfill my intentions
- To thrive
- Be seen, heard, understood, validated and celebrated

I make space in this world to _____; in all moments.
I remove all blockages to _____; in all moments.
I open all portals to _____; in all moments.
I stretch my capacity to _____, in all moments.
I am centered and empowered in _____, in all moments.
I resonate, emanate and am interconnected with all life in _____; in all moments.

THE ENERGETIC CLEANSE

NERGETIC CLEANSE
Think of something that annoys you or you have been obsessing over. It can be a job, person, task, relationship, global issue or a habit. After you name the issue, say each statement out-loud three times while tapping on the top of your head, and say it a fourth time while tapping on your chest.

"All engrams of _____ are removed; in all moments."

"All vivaxes with_____ are removed; in all moments."

"All tentacles of _____ are removed; in all moments."

"All my energy is withdrawn from _____; in all moments."

"All dependency on _____ is released; in all moments."

"Feeling beholden to _____ is eliminated; in all moments."

"All vows and agreements with _____ are recanted; in all moments.

"All contracts with _____ are nullified; in all moments."

"All curses with _____ are removed; in all moments."

"All blessings with _____ are removed; in all moments."

"All strings and cords with _____ are severed; in all moments."

"All karmic ties with _____ are dissolved; in all moments."

"All the pain, burden, limitations and engrams that _____ has inflicted are removed; in all moments."

"All the pain, burden, limitations and engrams that have been caused due to _____ are removed; in all moments."

"All that was taken from _____ is returned; in all moments."

"All the Joy, Love, Abundance, Freedom, Health, Success, Security, Companionship, Creativity, Peace, Life, Wholeness, Beauty, Enthusiasm, Contentment, Spirituality, Enlightenment and Confidence that _____ has taken is returned; in all moments."

"Resonating with _____ is released; in all moments."

"Emanating with _____ is released; in all moments."

"All of _____ is removed from my Sound Frequency; in all moments."

"All of _____ is removed from my Light Emanation; in all moments."

"My paradigm is shifted from _____ to Joy, Love, Abundance, Freedom, Health, Success, Security, Companionship, Creativity, Peace, Life, Wholeness, Beauty, Enthusiasm, Contentment, Spirituality, Enlightenment and Confidence; in all moments."

"All illusion is stripped from _____; in all moments."

"The first cause of enabling _____ is eliminated; in all moments."

"All masks, walls and armor are removed from _____; in all moments."

"All masks, walls and armor that were implemented due to _____ are removed; in all moments."

"All energy matrices of _____ are sent into the Light and Sound; in all moments."

189

"All complex energy matrices of _____ are escorted into the Light and Sound; in all moments."

"All portals to _____ are collapsed and dissolved; in all moments."

"All of _____ is transcended; in all moments."

"The Wei Chi of all bodies is repaired; in all moments."

"All bodies are aligned; in all moments."

"All are centered and empowered in Divine Love; in all moments."

GLOSSARY OF TERMS

There are some very complicated metaphysical concepts that do not need to be so difficult to understand. Anything that is fathomable in the Universe should be able to be simplified so a child can understand them. For instance, there are no words that explain the energy pull between two things. That would be the word vivaxes. As we become more enlightened, we will need more and more words to explain our ever-expanding relationship with energy.

Claws: Sometimes and in some instances, one will feel psychically gripped by an issue. The best way to depict the feeling of this is with the word claws.

Engrams: Engrams are the way that past issues are stored in our energy field. Think of how a groove in a vinyl record plays a song repeatedly when a needle is inserted in the groove. An engram is a groove in your energy field that plays a behavior repeatedly.

Enlightenment: The formula process of meeting all of the negativity within you and stripping it away so one is no longer at the mercy of the ego and sees one more as a reflection of the higher realms than in reactionary mode.

Light Bodies: We seem like solid energy. But we are really made of layers of energy consisting of different vibrations. Our physical body is the coarsest. Then the emotions create a layer of vibration around that. People know that layer as the astral level of vibration. Then there is the level that contains the memory of every past experience. This layer is called the causal plane and the records are called the akashic records. After that layer of vibration is the mental realm. This is the same layer as the ego and it is why it is difficult to see beyond the mental realm because the ego tries to prevent it. Above that level, the duality of the lower vibrations is dropped and then energy beyond that is one of such purity, it registers as a neutrality. That is why feeling good is not the highest expression of love, but loving neutrality or detachment is a more spiritual state. The ego will convey this as bliss but in its true state, it is neither positive nor negative.

Light Emanation: We are not solid matter. In energy, we are a light emanation and a sound frequency woven together to give the illusion of matter.

Matrix (pl. matrices): Stagnant energy can exist in cloud form. We walk through it all the time during the day. It can affect our moods. If we walk through energy and it identifies with our vibration, it may collect in us as individuals and seem like an intrusion.

Complex Energy Matrix: When an energy matrix intrudes upon your energy system and identifies itself with a personality. It may convince you and it that it is an aspect of you or that it is a totally different individual that has taken you over in some way. It is merely stagnant energy that needs to be dissipated. No melodrama necessary. Just release it with the taps.

Portal: An energetic gateway.

Psychic Stream of Energy: A compilation of a similar vibration of thoughts and emotions that creates a cloud-like energy that can affect those who are subjected to it.

Sound Frequency: One of the two aspects of ourselves, the other one being Light emanation. All energy is either Light or Sound. Knowing ourselves as Sound Frequencies and Light Emanations is breaking ourselves down to our true state devoid of ego and ego limitations. It is as a Sound Frequency or Light Emanation that we are capable of traveling in all realms and knowing ourselves as Omniscient, Omnipotent and Omnipresent. It is also a means of communicating with Source or God in Its native tongue.

Strings: When two energy sources touch, a string of connecting energy is formed between them. If attention is kept on this string, it can become reinforced with obsessive or repetitive thoughts. These strings need to be broken if one is going to be free of the object of the taps.

Tentacle: Energy that reaches out and attaches to someone perhaps to take from them or feed off their energy.

Vivaxis: An energy pull between two or more people, places or things.

Vortex: A vortex is an energy pull similar to a gravitational pull between two components. For example, there is a vortex between the sun and all the planets and there is a vortex between the earth and moon.

Wei Chi: The "skin" on the surface of your energy field that provides a natural barrier to energies interrupting your natural function. It gets pierced and broken during trauma and then it is more difficult for an energy to hold its electromagnetic charge. Someone whose Wei Chi is intact may have a natural magnetism.

www.jenuinehealing.com/sft-dictionary/

ABOUT THE AUTHOR

Jen Ward is an Ascended Master. This entails being a Reiki Master, gifted healer, inspirational speaker, author of many books and an innovator of a healing modality for self-empowerment. She offers a simple but dynamic protocol to assist individuals in clearing up all their energy imbalances (karma) with every person, experience, belief system and the Universe. She enables all those struggling, to cross the bridge of self-discovery, with her encouragement and instruction. Her passion is to empower the world by encouraging all individuals in their own miraculous healing adventure.

Jen is considered a sangoma, a traditional African shaman who channels ancestors, and clears energy by emoting sounds and vocalizations. An interesting prerequisite to being a sangoma is to have survived being on the brink of death. When it was first revealed that Jen was a sangoma, she had not yet fulfilled the rigorous prerequisites necessary. However, in April 2008, through a series of traumas, she returned to civilization meeting all the requirements. She passed through the transforming process of enlightenment. She returned to the world of humanity a devout soul inspired to serve.

Jen currently works diligently in the physical world and in the worlds of energy to assist all souls to reach greater heights of awareness and empowerment. Those who believe they have 'arrived,' may be the most entrenched in the mental realms. They can painlessly free themselves without relinquishing the comfort of their current belief system. All that needs to be released will fall away naturally. "Fear, in all its subtle forms of denial and judgment, will naturally fall away."

Many people report receiving healing assistance from Jen or

protection in the dream state and even more subtle realms. Jen is passionate to shatter the mentality of sitting at the feet of another. She shares truth and wisdom graciously and abundantly. Jen makes the practice of doling out truth in increments to set up the dynamic of personality worship obsolete. Her passion is to assist the world over the brink of all perceived limitations, beyond the mind's scope, into the realms of enlightenment.

Enlightenment Unveiled: Expound into Empowerment: This book contains case studies to help you peel away the layers to your own empowerment using the tapping technique.

Grow Where You Are Planted: Quotes for an Enlightened Jeneration: Inspirational quotes that are seeds to shift your consciousness into greater awareness.

Perpetual Calendar: Daily Exercises to Maintain Balance and Harmony in Your Health, Relationships and the Entire World: 369 days of powerful taps to use as a daily grounding practice for those who find meditation difficult.

Children of the Universe. Poetry to Elevate the Reader to the 5th Dimension: Passionate prose to lead the reader lovingly into expanded consciousness.

Letters of Accord: Assigning Words to Unspoken Truth: Truths that the ancient ones want you to know to redirect your life and humanity back into empowerment.

The Do What You Love Diet: Finally, Finally, Finally, Feel Good in Your Own Skin: Revolutionary approach to regaining fitness by tackling primal imbalances in relationship to food.

Emerging from the Mist: Awakening the Balance of Female Empowerment in the World: Release all the issues that prevent someone from embracing their female empowerment.

Affinity for All Life: Valuing Your Relationship with All Species: This book is a means to strengthen and affirm your relationship with the animal kingdom.

The Wisdom of the Trees: If one is struggling for purpose, they can find love, and truth by tuning into the Wisdom of the Trees.

Chronicles of Truth: Truth has been buried away for way too long. Here is a means to discover the truth that lies dormant within yourself.

Healing Your Relationships: This book is a means to open up communications and responsiveness to others so that clarity and respect can flourish again in society.

How to Awaken Your Inner Dragon: Visualizations to Empower Yourself and the World: Tap into the best possible version of you and the world.

Collecting Everyday Miracles: Commit to Being Empowered: This book is a thought provoking means to recreate the moment of conception with everyday miracles. It is through gratitude and awareness. This is what this book fosters.

The SFT Lexicon: Spiritual Freedom Technique: Tap into the powerful ability of the mind to self-heal.

Past Lives, Dreams and Inspiration: People are starving for truth. Unfortunately, they have been conditioned to dismiss their dreams and all remnants of past lives in discovering their own trajectory connection to truth. This book gives life to the expansiveness of self-discovery through one's past lives and dream experiences. There is no greater form of inspiration than discovering one's own depth.

2018 -- A Turning Point: Shift from Primal Mode to Enlightenment: If in 2018 you sensed a shift in the world, if you sensed an internal struggle happening on the world's behalf, if you are fascinated with truths that are hidden from the masses, or if you have some programming left that you would like to eliminate, this book is for you.

God: The Ultimate Search Engine: Finally, a book to address all the layers of shame piled on the individual in the name of a vengeful, petty God. Man has spoken for God long enough. It's time to speak to God directly.

Manifest Wealth and Abundance: This book removes all the blockages that individuals have put in their own way in accepting abundance and trusting it to flow.

All of Jen's books can be found on her website at www.JenuineHealing.com.

www.ingramcontent.com/pod-product-compliance
Lightning Source LLC
Chambersburg PA
CBHW051421090426
42737CB00014B/2769